6-7-75

THEY CAME BY SEA

THEY CAME

A Pictorial History

by

THE WARD RITCHIE PRESS AND THE MARITIME MUSEUM

BY SEA

of San Diego Bay

Jerry MacMullen

ASSOCIATION OF SAN DIEGO · 1969

To: Don M. Stewart

As an officer of command rank in the old Naval Militia of California he saw wartime service in the North Atlantic convoys — and made men of some pretty wild kids. He has served his community faithfully as a City Councilman, as City Treasurer and as Postmaster. And now, in his ninety-sixth year, he still carries on with vigor the unending battle for truth in the chronicling of the history of the West.

PREFACE

This is not a history of San Diego Bay in terms of change-of-command ceremonies nor of civic banquets; it will not tell you about the social significance of the tuna industry nor will it supply tables of statistics on cargoes or the revenue from tidelands leases. Rather, it will try to plug up some of the holes left by those who, in bygone years, apparently felt that nothing of interest occurred from the arrival of the sea-borne elements of Don Gaspar de Portolá's expedition in 1769 until the Navy began to fly cloth-and-bamboo aeroplanes on North Island. It is just as well to face the fact that "New" San Diego was brought in, piece by piece, in sailing vessels and lumbering sidewheelers, and that bellying canvas played an important part in the town's economy for many years.

In that now wraith-like fleet were sturdy wooden medium clippers out of Searsport and Bath; iron and steel ships and barks hailing from Dundee and Liverpool and Havre and Bremen — and from London and Trondhjem and Barry. They brought steaming coal from New South Wales and blacksmith coal (which had to be watched for spontaneous combustion) from Pennsylvania; they brought steel and glass and cement from Continental Europe, and there was a veritable armada of small schooners from the "dog-holes" of Northern California's Mendocino coast, with redwood from which to build a city. From time to time empty Cape Horners would load San Diego County grain from rolling fields which today grow dense with split-level homes, for the brewers of Germany. Up from the Lower Coast, as the Mexican waters were called, came the tiny schooners and big sloops of the "Mosquito Fleet" with sea-otter pelts and with orchilla and seal-oil, and gold and copper ore. The tall ships and their lusty crews came and went and were quickly forgotten; everyone was too busy telling and re-telling the story of California's missions, and of the Romantic Days of the Dons. So do not be surprised if the following pages lay emphasis on sail and on the coastwise steamers, and pick up such forgotten items as the day when the Navy discovered that you could at last get a battleship into San Diego Bay — or why the tug had to be towed home by the schooner.

Gathering material has not been easy. Half a century ago a tape recorder, in the hands of anyone who recognized the passing of a phase of history which had lasted for thousands of years, would have been all but priceless. Now we have the electronic gear, but most of the characters have made their last landfall these many years ago. In the early days there were no formal port records kept and local newspaper files are indexed only up through 1879, and then from 1930 on, which eliminates most of San Diego's lusty days of sail. Nothing has turned up but a battered log-book started in 1888 by Capt. E. B. Dunnells, a port pilot, and it ends in 1902; it is aboard the museum-ship *Star of India,* and has been microfilmed by the San Diego Public Library.

[v]

The U. S. Custom House Barge Office had a file of the original "Boarding Books" which listed all foreign arrivals — name, rig, consignee, cargo — until that dark day in the mid-1930s when some Washington Jack-in-office passed through on an "efficiency" survey; he declared that they were taking up so many square feet of space at so many cents a foot, and ordered them burned, even though they had been promised to the local historical society. You may destroy excess government property, he growled, but it is a Federal offense if you give it away.

So many people have been so wonderfully helpful in picking up the loose ends before it is forever too late, that it has made the job a happy one. Don M. Stewart, who at past ninety wrote that lovely little autobiography called *Frontier Port*, made available his IBM-card memory — and thank Heaven that he spent his boyhood days prowling around the waterfront. The patient staff of the California Room and the Newspaper Room of the San Diego Public Library were priceless, and Larry Booth, who presides benignly over the Title Insurance & Trust Company's fabulous collection of early San Diego photos, rolled out the Red Rug. Bert Shankland performed miracles with terrible negatives, and gave gleaming nuggets of lore of the old Navy from his days in the armored cruiser *California*. Capt. Joe Brennan, son of a lighthouse-keeper and brother of the master of the *Harvard* — and who taught this writer how to steer the tug *Bahada* — supplied photos and personal accounts of great value. Unrecorded details of the local fisheries came from Joe Camillo and Matt Ghio and from Lawrence and Mary Oliver. The aid from Col. George Ruhlen was invaluable, as was that of Capt. Harry Krog, senior port pilot, and of the staff of the Unified Port District.

From around Los Angeles Dr. John Haskell Kemble, Robert Weinstein, Capt. Fred Klebingat and Everett and Anna Marie Hager gave generously of their time — as did Harry and Matilda Dring, Capt. Harold D. Huycke, Irene Simpson, Karl Kortum and Robert W. Parkinson of the San Francisco Bay area. In Washington, D. C., Dr. John Lyman, A. O. Anderson and Rear Adm. E. M. Eller were most helpful, as were those friendly people at the Penobscot Marine Museum of Searsport, Me., and the Mariners' Museum at Newport News, Va. Lee Strobel provided a first-hand account of that grisly July morning aboard the gunboat *Bennington*, while overseas the office of the U. S. Naval Attache in London got, from the British Admiralty, information of long-gone ships of Her Majesty's Navy. Rounding out the "Hands Across The Sea" category was help from the jovial Capt. Alan Villiers in Oxford, and Capt. R. Storrar Boyd in Dundee.

Without them all, this book could not have been written.

JERRY MacMullen

San Diego, California
February 22, 1969

CONTENTS

1. Sails from the South'ard

*In command was a certain Juan Rodriguez Cabrillo, a
Portuguese by birth and a skilled mariner.*
—CHARLES E. CHAPMAN

On September 28, 1542, the Portuguese navigator João Rodrigues Cabrilho
cautiously entered San Diego Bay while, hopefully, looking for China, and
thus became the first white man to set foot on the coast of what we now call
California. He named the bay San Miguel.

Possibly because he was sailing in the employ of the Spanish government,
Cabrilho's name has been altered to the Spanish form of Juan Rodriguez
Cabrillo—and that was not all that he suffered at the hands of the name-
changers. He went on, far up the California coast, and returned to winter
quarters at San Miguel Island, where he died early in January of 1543 from
an injury received while landing through the surf. And so far as Spain was
concerned, nothing was done about the newly discovered port for sixty years.

It is quite possible, however, that another Portuguese navigator sailing
for Spain, may have visited San Diego Bay late in 1595; this would have been
Sebastian Cermenho, sailing down the coast in a home-made launch after
losing his ship, a Manila galleon, at Drake's Bay. Cermenho, regrettably,
incurred the enmity of the good merchants of Acapulco by losing that galleon, which was all full of goodies from Manila for what may well have been
the January Sales at Acapulco. And the merchants had the ear of the viceroy.
Although he had been ordered to survey the coast on his way home from
Manila and was trying to do so with a vessel which was clumsy and wholly
unsuited for such work, he caught hell for losing her and the viceroy gun-
decked his reports; they have never been found.

Before rising to command of a galleon, Cermenho had been pilot in one
of them—the *Santa Ana* or, as people liked to call her, "The Great Saint Ann";
one of his shipmates in that hapless craft was a cheerful extrovert named
Sebastian Vizcaíno. That was in 1587, and it was their hard luck to fall afoul
of young Thomas Cavendish, down around Cape San Lucas at the tip of Baja
California. Back in England he was called a "Gentleman Adventurer" but
he was known elsewhere, and more realistically, as a pirate. Before looting
and firing the *Santa Ana*, however, he was decent enough to put her people
ashore with a supply of wine and dried beans, and even a bit of lumber and

[1]

old sails for rigging up a crude shelter. While most of the survivors were running around wringing their hands and calling upon all the saints in the calendar to please do something about it, Vizcaíno got busy. From the burned hulk (which luckily had drifted ashore) and that lumber and canvas, he fashioned a weird ship in which, with Cermenho's aid, he landed them safely in Acapulco.

Time was marching on. Having thought it over for a matter of some sixty years, the Spanish brass decided that it might be in order to send someone up the coast to re-check the Cabrilho survey—and Vizcaíno, now a prominent figure around Acapulco, applied for the job. Over the screams of the viceroy, who regarded him as a bit of a blow-hard, he got the assignment and set out in 1602. One of his orders was that he was not to change any of the names given to the bays and islands and capes by Cabrilho—but on the flimsy pre-text that the navigation and descriptions left by his predecessor were so bad that he could recognize little if anything from them, he changed just about all of those original names. That is why today it is San Diego and not San Miguel.

The Cabrilho-Vizcaíno gap of sixty years was nothing compared to the next one, which was nearly three times as long. It wasn't until early in 1769 that headquarters in New Spain, having heard vague rumors of Russian or even English designs on the long coastline which Spain had discovered, sent three ships out from La Paz, just up the Gulf of California coast from Cape San Lucas. They were part of a land-sea expedition under Don Gaspar de Portolá; he would go overland to meet them at San Diego, where he would establish a military post and then do the same thing at Monterey. Of the trio the smallest, the *San José*, cleared La Paz and was never seen again. Another, the *San Antonio,* made San Diego April 11, 1769, 54 days out. The flagship *San Carlos* got there 17 days later—but she had left sooner, and her time was 110 days. And she was in terrible shape. Scurvy and shortage of water had taken their toll; the pilot and the coxswain of the launch had died and the rest were so weak that Capt. Vicente Vila had to call upon men from the anchored *San Antonio* for help in furling his sails.

Vila moved his tottering crew of zombies ashore and set up a crude camp on the beach; anything was better than the cramped quarters aboard the ship in which they had spent nearly four months. There they stayed until May 14, when the first units of the land party arrived under Capt. Fernando de Rivera y Moncada of the Spanish Army. He promptly moved them to what now is called Presidio Hill, overlooking today's Old Town, and started the perma-nent if crude construction of a military post.

San Diego had been, albeit tenuously, secured. Portolá arrived July 1 and was followed the next day by Fr. Junípero Serra, that indefatigable Francis-can priest who, on July 16, founded the Mission San Diego de Alcalá, first of the twenty-one missions of Alta California. Officially, this has come to be accepted as the day on which civilization in California began, and for many years the name of Rivera was forgotten in San Diego. All but forgotten, too, were the names of Portolá—and of Lt. Pedro Fages who commanded three ships, two of which got to San Diego ahead of everyone else.

Spanish rule was to last for some 52 years, and then Mexico would take over for a quarter of a century. San Diego's essential supplies would come in by the yearly transport from San Blas until 1810 when, with internal difficulties increasing everywhere, New Spain had other worries, and the scheduled service ended. Those San Blas supply ships would be better, more dependable than Fages' craft—for by now men realized that the lines of a vessel's underbody were more important than the elegance of the heraldic and religious emblems emblazoned on her sails. The tiller and the whipstaff would give way to the steering-wheel, and the octant would replace the astrolabe. Capt. George Vancouver would visit San Diego, enjoy the hospitality of mission and presidio—and his blunt observations on the port's vulnerability would lead to the building of Fort Guijarros, San Diego's first harbor-defense post and the only one ever to fire a shot in anger.

Meanwhile the hide-ships and the fast-dealing Yankee traders were climbing up over the horizon, in steadily increasing numbers.

2. Fast-Buck Boys from Out-of-Town

At sunset on the second day, we had a large and well wooded headland before us, behind which lay the little harbor of San Diego.

—RICHARD HENRY DANA JR.

No vessel could have had a better-sounding name than the Yankee brig *Betsy*, Capt. Charles Winship, for introducing the American merchant marine to the unsuspecting Spanish authorities at San Diego; it gave a clam-chowder and baked-beans atmosphere of simple integrity to the whole thing and makes all the more regrettable the subsequent conduct of one of her officers. From a Public Relations standpoint, they should have left First Mate Joseph O'Cain at home.

There is no recorded unpleasantness about the visit of the *Betsy* on August 25, 1800, nor of the ship *Enterprise*— Ezekiel Hubbell, master—which came in during June of 1801. During the eighteen months which elapsed before another Yankee appeared, the Spaniards had been lulled into a false sense of security, so when the ship *Alexander* showed up on February 26, 1803, they accepted her skipper's statements at their face value; he had been beset by storms, repairs were urgently needed, his crew was half dead from scurvy and they were down to only a demijohn or so of water. After five days in port, however, the authorities found that instead of getting themselves and their ship in order, the *Alexander's* people had been loading her up with sea-otter pelts, obtained from wily Indians and from underpaid soldiers. This being contrary to Spanish law, the *Alexander* and her mendacious crew were promptly and properly booted out to sea.

The *Alexander* was gone but a fortnight when more bad news appeared, this time in the form of the brig *Lelia Byrd*, Capt. William Shaler. Perhaps

Overly dignified by the term "Battle of San Diego Bay", the escape of the hijacking Lelia Byrd *was, nonetheless, a fair little bit of cannonry back in 1803, until the impudent Yankee silenced the Spanish fort; an impression of how things looked, that day, off Ballast Point.*—
OIL ON CANVAS, BY THE AUTHOR

because they didn't lay it on quite so heavily about the dying crew and all that, the Spaniards let them come in for water and firewood—but they were to deal with no one but the *comandante* himself, and they weren't even to think about sea-otter pelts. Nevertheless, it wasn't long before that, in addition to getting otter-skins from the Indians, they had corrupted a corporal of cannoneers who knew where there was a nice cache of pelts—the private racket of no one less than the *comandante* himself. The work-party sent ashore to get them was seized—but the alert men who had remained aboard the brig overpowered the armed guard which had been placed there, got ashore, and rescued their shipmates.

Now the fat was really in the fire. The *Lelia Byrd* either must surrender ignominiously or make a run for it—which meant sailing close to the guns of Fort Guijarros, on Ballast Point. With the first morning breeze they loosed their sails, catted the anchor and stood out toward sea—and the Spanish fort opened fire. Like all other well-regulated merchantmen of her time, the *Lelia Byrd* had her own guns, and although she suffered both hull and rigging damage in the encounter, she silenced the fort with what, for want of a better term, might be called a broadside. Once clear of the harbor, she hove-to only long enough to put her disarmed Spanish guard over the side in a small boat, and wish them bon voyage.

It is small wonder that when, a few months later, the ship *O'Cain* appeared, the Spanish authorities wouldn't even let her come in. Her master was Capt. Joseph O'Cain, our old friend from the *Betsy*, and in the interim he had met some interesting people, not the least of whom was Alexander Baranov, the No. 1 Russian in Alaska. The two had made a deal: In the sea-otter field, Baranov would rob the Spaniards blind as far south as Santa Barbara, where O'Cain and his ilk would take over. Later they would meet at Kodiak and divide up the loot.

Undaunted by his chilly reception at San Diego, O'Cain stood on to the south, finally coming to an anchor at San Quintín. Swift riders meanwhile had brought word of O'Cain to the *comandante* of the nearest outpost—but he was a kindly man and, in spite of his orders, he was completely taken in by O'Cain's pitiful routine about the scurvy and the dying sailors and all the rest. He should have known better.

After the good ship *O'Cain* had been hanging around for some four months, it gradually dawned upon the *comandante* that perhaps everything was not strictly kosher. And sure enough, when he went down to the beach, there were otter-skins piled up, all over the place; the *O'Cain's* dying crew, which included a force of Aleut fur-hunters, had not been idle. While some of the Yankees and Aleuts (they were all armed to the teeth) chased off the Spanish Army's token force, the rest of them loaded up the pelts, some 1,100 of them, and they sailed for Alaska, to report to Papa Baranov.

Although some of his pug-uglies got two years in jail at San Pedro in 1814— they had made the mistake of adding cattle-stealing to their repertoire—

[6]

O'Cain continued to plague the Spaniards for a few years longer. By that time he and his mob had all but exterminated the sea-otter, and hunting them no longer was an attractive proposition.

From 1800 to 1828 there were 31 merchant ship arrivals at San Diego and 16 of them were American; of the other 15, six were Russian, four British, three Hawaiian, one Spanish and one French. Although the first Yankee hide-ship to visit the Pacific Coast—the *Sachem*, Capt. Henry Gyzelaar—showed up in 1822 from Boston, she did not visit San Diego until 1825, and the *Arab* and the *Mentor* had come in the year before. The trade in California hides was growing, and in 1829 the first of the hide-houses at La Playa was built, to take care of a cargo of hides for the *Brookline;* her mate, James P. Arther was left in charge. He is credited with raising the first American flag in San Diego if not in fact in all of California, and the event occurred either in 1828 or 1829, for he had been here in 1828 as mate of the ship *Harbinger*, of Boston. The flag was home-made and was displayed on the occasion of the arrival of the Hawaiian schooner *Washington*—or the arrival of a British man-o-war, depending upon whose story you happen to prefer. Manuel Rodriguez, the Mexican *comandante*, was terribly upset about it, and rode down to La Playa in person, on his best Sunday horse, to inform those tactless Yankees that there would be no more of that.

Regardless of how many hundreds of hides were stowed in a hide-ship or how many barrels of oil were aboard a whaler, the brig *Pilgrim*, of Boston, was historically the most important of them all, for it was the *Pilgrim* which brought Richard Henry Dana to San Diego in 1835 and thus got the place into that all-time classic of the sea, *Two Years Before the Mast.* For generations, people read that book, unaware of the fact that they were being short-changed. It seems that some pious busybodies edited Dana's work rather heavily, excising those passages which had to do with the frequently sulphurous diction of the *Pilgrim's* people, various forms of trick and device while getting to windward of the Mexican Customs Service, and such touching scenes as the one of the priest coming home by burro, so utterly stoned that it's a wonder he was able to hang on. In 1961 Dr. John Haskell Kemble, Professor of History at Pomona College, got hold of the original MSS., and the result was a two-color history; what Dana's relatives and do-gooder friends had left in is printed in black, while the "undesirable" text, put back by Dr. Kemble, is in brown ink.

Some of those brown-ink passages are lovely.

3. The Gringo Takes Over

The entrance to San Diego Bay lies about 10 miles northwestward from the boundary between the United States and Mexico.

—SAILING DIRECTIONS

It was only natural that the area around the old hide-houses should be the location for the first American activities of the Port of San Diego. The first U. S. Custom House was built there and La Playa thus became a contender as the locale for the new town which everyone realized must come some day, on the shores of the bay instead of at the foot of Presidio Hill.

When the Army decided to erect a barracks at San Diego, a shipload of lumber was sent to La Playa, with a young Quartermaster officer in charge. Meanwhile, however, William Heath Davis, who had been trading in to San Diego since he was a boy, had started a town project in the area around what now is the foot of Market Street. He and his associates persuaded the youthful lieutenant that the Davis location was a far better place, so the lumber was loaded aboard again and brought up the bay to a spot which Davis, in laying out his new town, had set aside for Army use; it was here that San Diego Barracks was built in 1851, and stood for seventy years. Even this shot-in-the-arm, however, failed to alter the course of history, and what came to be known as "Davis' Folly" faded away; it was not until Alonzo Erastus Horton arrived in 1868 that moving San Diego down to the edge of the bay was promoted in dead earnest, and successfully.

By now the steamboat had arrived and was here to stay. An Act of Congress passed March 3, 1847, specified that steamers of the subsidised Pacific Mail Steamship Company were to make San Diego, Monterey and San Francisco to pick up and discharge mail, and their first steamer, the spanking-new *California*, which left New York late in the autumn of 1848, was supposed to call but didn't. Approaching San Diego on the night of February 20-21, 1849, she found herself dangerously low on coal, and instead of risking the few extra miles into and out of the harbor, she just kept on, using her sails and burning up some of her interior woodwork—until they remembered a few tons of coal, overstowed with cargo, and more or less triumphantly steamed into San Francisco. What probably was the first steamer to enter San Diego Bay was Pacific Mail's *Oregon*, on March 30, 1849. Having picked up some dubious coal at San Blas, she had no excuse for passing up San Diego as the *California* had done. She stayed in port for half an hour, strictly for the purpose of legally carrying out her mail contract.

And that brings us to San Diego's first fuelling facility—the bark *Clarissa Andrews*, which came here about 1852 and for the next few years lay off La Playa, serving as a coal-hulk for Pacific Mail. No spring chicken by then, she was built at Salisbury, Mass., in 1831 and was only 124 feet long. The immortal Lt. George Horatio Derby—Army engineer and, some insist, the father of American humorous writing—speaks of her as "... the bark *Clarissa Andrews* (filled with coal for the P. M. S. S. Co.), wherein dwells Captain Bogart like a second Robinson Crusoe with a man Friday who is mate, steward and all hands." This was Capt. J. C. Bogart, who first saw San Diego in 1834 from the deck of the ship *Black Warrior* and who in 1853 became San Diego's first State Senator; the "man Friday" was Capt. Samuel Warren Hackett, whilom New England (and California) whaleman; later he shone as one of Southern California's most famous stagecoach drivers. The *Clarissa Andrews* served as a coal-hulk and landing-stage until around 1856, when she went on the beach in a storm. A one-time Army mule-skinner called "Squire" A. S. Ensworth, who later became a judge and a pretty good one at that, salvaged timbers from her to build a house in rural Spring Valley. The house, later occupied by the noted historian Hubert Howe Bancroft, is preserved as a State Historical Landmark.

And now the little trickle of shipping was beginning to swell slightly. Pacific Mail was making its regular stops, and as early as 1850 an advertisement in the *Daily Alta California* of San Francisco announced that freight and passengers would be accepted by the brig *Placer* for Monterey, San Pedro and San Diego. Construction of the first lighthouse in Southern California was started near the tip of Point Loma in 1854, and that meant a small boost in traffic—for the lighthouse would need bricks and lumber and sash and at long last the beautifully faceted lens which, like everything else which was used in San Diego, had to come by sea. Until the completion of the first railroad to the north in 1882, the town depended upon communication by ship or stagecoach—and from the pueblo of San Diego to that of Los Angeles by coach took two days, unless a highwayman or a broken axle made it take longer.

A newspaper, *The San Diego Herald*, blossomed forth in 1853, but it consisted largely of San Francisco ads. Little two-masters, and the infrequent steamers, were San Diego's feeble link with civilization, and news of the outside world came chiefly from bundles of San Francisco newspapers, brought to the *Herald's* editor by the obliging purser of the *Goliah* or the *California* or the *Constitution*.

Finally the aggressive Horton came to San Diego, and the truly pastoral days of a flea-bitten little hamlet were on their way out.

·Lying at Culverwell's Wharf in the early 1870s is Pacific Mail's side-wheeler California,
She was built in 1848, visited San Diego for the first time a year later, and paid her last
call in the autumn of 1874. Her engines were removed in 1875 and, still under the same
name, she became a three-masted bark; she was sold foreign in 1895. The little schooner
is the Dorinda, for many years a trader to the Lower Coast.—HISTORICAL COLLECTION, TITLE
INSURANCE & TRUST CO.

4. The Glory Days of Sail

This was the world's worst headland, bleak outpost of sailors' misery and wretched memory. This was Cape Horn!

—ALAN VILLIERS

Having contributed a minor footnote to history by being the only California clipper to call at San Diego, the *Stillwell S. Bishop* loosed her sails and stood out past Point Loma on June 24, 1854 bound for Benicia, which she reached eight days later.

Her record of 112 days from New York to San Diego still stands, so far as the Cape Horners go; it would be another 27 years before a ship would come to San Diego direct from New York, and in those years ships would become both bigger and slower. She had Army supplies for San Diego and Benicia which meant, so far as San Diego was concerned, both for the local garrison and for the sweltering frontier outposts which lay beyond the mountains to the eastward.

Coastal sailing-vessels and the steamers of Pacific Mail continued to make their well-spaced visits, and when Horton started to build the town where it should have been in the first place, the tempo increased. Lush stands of redwood to the north of San Francisco were producing abundant lumber, slid down improvised chutes to schooners moored at the foot of Mendocino's forbidding cliffs, and what San Diego needed was sailed down from there. The "Tom Scott Boom" of the early 1870s, sparked by the fact that the Texas & Pacific actually started to build a transcontinental rail line in to San Diego, came and went—but the forces which it set in motion would continue, railroad or not. Even in the economic doldrums there would be need for a certain amount of lumber, of San Francisco hardware and notions, of coal-oil for the lamps.

It was the hey-day of little two-masters like the *Dashing Wave* and the *Bobolink* and the *Lillebonne*, which were about as big as anyone would dare to use while fooling around such now forgotten "Redwood Coast" out-

---

Queenstown for orders! In this striking view by Herbert R. Fitch the grain-ship Sierra Estrella *is leaving San Diego on Nov. 2, 1897; the tow-line has gone slack and the man in the Whitehall boat is about to take off the pilot.*—HISTORICAL COLLECTION, TITLE INSURANCE & TRUST CO.

ports as Whitesboro or Bowen's Landing. There you anchored, let your stern swing in almost to the white water at the foot of the cliffs, and got your lumber by a "rough-and-ready" wooden chute, or slid down a wire cable. It was no place for a big ship. What may well have been the first three-masted schooner in the timber trade to San Diego was the *A. P. Jordan,* which arrived in mid-April of 1869 from Puget Sound with pine lumber for Louis Rose—after whom Point Loma's Roseville is named—and rafted it ashore at La Playa.

But massive timbers were going to be needed also, for wharves and for bridges, and that meant pine from Puget Sound and the Columbia—and the lumber trade out of Humboldt Bay was growing also. So three-masters began to appear with greater frequency, as did brigs and brigantines, barkentines, barks and even full-rigged ships. The first four-masted schooner to call at San Diego was the brand-new *Wm. F. Witzemann* on July 23, 1887.

Tom Scott's efforts with the T. & P. had failed, but in 1881 work started on the California Southern Railroad, building north from National City on upper San Diego Bay, to connect with the transcontinental line at Colton and by-pass Los Angeles. California Southern would have a voracious appetite for ties from Northern California, bridge-timbers too big to handle in a tiny schooner, steel rails from Europe (along with cement and coke and patent fertilizers for the town's growing urban and rural economy) and for coal, coal—and more coal. Some of this would come from England and some from British Columbia, but the bulk of it eventually would be up from Australia and New Zealand.

It was their larger and hence more economical cargo-capacity, as well as hatches big enough to take long timbers, which brought the Down Easters into the San Diego lumber trade. The little *Adelaide,* in from Whitesboro in the spring of 1885, had only 170,000 board-feet of lumber; the full-rigged ship *State of Maine* would lay down a 1,000,000-foot cargo three years later, but definitely not from an outport like Whitesboro.

San Diego's first steam locomotive arrived in the brig *Orient* on July 9, 1881; it had been brought overland to San Francisco and the last leg of the journey, by sea, took a leisurely five days; the tiny 0-4-0 switcher was lovingly accompanied by its engineer, a Mr. Xander, who soon busied himself putting the pieces together. Three more California Southern locomotives would come in Sept. 3 in the *James A. Wright,* 147 days from New York by way of Cape Horn. In 1967 Don M. Stewart, pioneer San Diegan, recalled seeing her, sailing up to National City in the moonlight; he was eight years old at the time. It's funny, the little details of a picture which will stick in a kid's mind to be recalled, crystal-clear, scores of years later—like the foggy morning in 1884 when he stood on the Court House lawn and heard, from the direction of the bay, a muted "Tut-tut-tut-tut-tut-tut! Tut-tut-tut-tut-tut-tut! Tut-tut-tut-tut-tut-tut!"—the splashing paddles of the side-wheeler *Orizaba*—or was it the *Ancon?* as she came up the bay.

And already the big Cape Horners—iron and steel ships and barks from Europe—were on their way. It was a big event in San Diego when the first of them came in, and a big ship as well; the day was Aug. 7, 1881, and she was the handsome four-masted full-rigged ship *Trafalgar*, Capt. Duncan Johnston, of Glasgow. With more than 2,000 tons of railroad iron, she had made it in 118 days from Antwerp—a record which would stand until 1903 when the British four-masted bark *Vanduara* clipped three days off of it. There were others in her wake, all with material to be used by California Southern's gangs of Chinese track-layers. There was the big iron ship *Mac-Millan*, flying the Blue Ensign of the Royal Naval Reserve, and the *Duke of Argyll*, the *Carnegie*, the *Lady Lisgar* and the *Alumina*, the Bluenose ship *Connaught* and the bark *Lizzie Perry;* for some of them, it would be anything but a pleasure-trip. A hurricane took everything off of the *Lizzie Perry* but the stump of her mainmast, and she had to put in at Montevideo for repairs; similar mishaps sent the *Lady Lisgar* in to Rio, and the *Duke of Argyll* to Port Stanley en route.

At no time has a Cape Horn passage been a thing to dismiss lightly, and when the *Duke of Argyll* made San Diego on Nov. 13, 1882, she ended a 16-month voyage from Europe which was an epic of frustration and misery. After loading 13,000 steel rails at Antwerp she had gone to Newport, Wales, to top off with 50 tons of corrugated iron, and when she sailed on July 16, 1881, Capt. J. Handyside had no warning of what lay ahead.

It started when she hit a full gale on Oct. 8 and her foremast went, damaging some of the main lower rigging in its fall. Partial repairs were made as the ship—now, one might say, reduced to a brig—stumbled on. Then came another gale, and on Oct. 17 a main topmast backstay snapped; down came the mainmast and, shortly afterward, the mizzen. With great difficulty they cleared up the mess the next day (the log for Oct. 18 reads ". . . Ship labouring heavily and shipping large bodies of water . . .") and rigged a jury mainmast. Captain Handyside now altered course for the Falkland Islands and on Nov. 7 they made Port Stanley. There they found another San Diego-bound refugee, the *Alumina*, which had come in Nov. 1, her cargo having shifted.

Word was sent back to the owners, but it was months before new spars for the *Duke of Argyll* arrived. Her cargo had to be removed into a hulk alongside and subsequently re-loaded, but repairs finally were completed and she got away Aug. 22, 1881, making San Diego 84 days later. The *Alumina* had left March 10, but her troubles were not over, and by May her people—including Capt. Thomas Jones' wife and four-year-old daughter—were on definitely short rations. On June 6, with provisions practically gone, they spoke the British ship *Lastingham*, London for San Francisco, and got what they thought was sufficient to take them on to San Diego. It proved to be a miscalculation, and when they sailed in exactly a month later, they were practically starving.

Into San Diego's modest Cape Horn trade would come other ships, of other flags, although the Red Duster would predominate among the overseas windjammers. There would be big German ships and barks, grey-hulled Frenchmen, and Norwegian, Swedish and other nationalities. Infrequent Yankee ships would arrive from the East Coast—but there would be many of them from the Pacific Northwest, with coal. A modest export trade in wheat and barley would build up, and there would be a steady string of ships with coal from Newcastle, N.S.W., and Wellington, N.Z., from the mid-1880s until after the turn of the century, when oil cut that traffic down to a trickle. The Cape Horners would bring cement and steel and patent fertilizer from England and Germany, glass from Belgium, and assorted lots of general cargo until 1914, when the British ship *Dudhope* landed the last cargo to San Diego by way of that classic route of the tall ships.

Completion of the railroad in 1885 put San Diego on the map at last. Eastern tourists and health-seekers, lured by the climate and by a railroad rate-war which finally brought the fare to California from the middle west down to $1, descended upon the town in hordes, both by rail and by coasting steamers—with even a few by sail. The railroad was gobbling up coal and the increasing tempo of a gigantic real-estate boom brought an explosive increase in building. In 1886, 90 vessels arrived with lumber—but there were 387 the following year; there were 42 arrivals from foreign ports in 1886, and 201 in 1887. At the same time steamer arrivals from San Francisco jumped from 109 to 308, dumping 60,152 passengers into a town not too well prepared to accommodate them. Twelve coal ships in 1886 brought 12,600 tons of fuel—and 30 such ships, the following year, landed a total of 54,000 tons.

In the winter of 1887-88, the hackneyed term "a forest of spars" was more than a mere figure of speech. On Nov. 1, 1887, the roster of vessels in port showed five full-rigged ships, eleven barks, a barkentine, seven schooners and eight steamers. Dockside space was at a premium, and many of them lay at anchor awaiting their turn—while their masters fumed and cursed at the delay and their sailors, singly and in groups, deserted for the fleshpots of that lusty part of San Diego known as Stingaree. Some 600 longshoremen were at work, aided by too-few donkey-engines. The last of the side-wheelers, the *Ancon*, was still paddling in and out from San Francisco, competing with slim-hulled iron steamers in bringing swarms of newcomers. And trains were puffing in, to unload bewildered tenderfeet into that part of California Southern's ornate Victorian station which was appropriately lettered "Immigrant Room." The Great Boom was approaching its crest.

And it was, of course, too good to last. Free-wheeling speculators over-did it, and in a matter of months San Diego was on the toboggan.

---

*On the following pages: Looking southeasterly from the tower of San Diego Barracks at Arctic and H Streets (now Kettner and Market) in the 1880s; the railroad track at the left is the old California Southern. In the foreground are squatters' shacks, while beyond lie the Russ Lumber and Pacific Coast Steamship Co.—formerly Horton's—wharves.—*HISTORICAL COLLECTION, TITLE INSURANCE & TRUST CO.

5. Mudflats and Long-legged Wharves

. . . in all directions rose the masts of ships, bewildering with the lace-work and tracery of rigging.
—W. CLARK RUSSELL

The first wharf worthy of the name was built by William Heath Davis in the summer of 1850— a T-wharf which ran out, south, from about what now would be the intersection of Pacific Highway and Market Street. Various ships used it, generally without bothering to pay Davis any wharfage, until it began to need repairs which neither Davis nor the free-loaders were willing to provide. The Pacific Mail and other steamers, which had shifted from La Playa back to the embryonic town, went back to the routine of bringing passengers in by a ship's boat until it grounded, and then piggy-backing them ashore on the shoulders of brawny mariners. The final blow came during the Civil War when soldiers stationed at San Diego Barracks to protect the modest hamlet from the Confederate Army, ran out of fuel and the people in Washington to whom they wrote about it didn't even bother to answer the letters. So they began taking up Davis' wharf for use both as fuel and for lumber which they needed but couldn't get. Davis put in a claim, but Congress sat on it for a score of years, and then paid him but a fraction of what was due him. The area of the wharf's base is known as Dead Men's Point or, more properly, Punta de los Muertos; the name was given in 1782 when a number of sailors from the Spanish survey party under Juan Pantoja y Arriaga were buried there, the victims of scurvy. At one time it also was called— at least by the editor of the *San Diego Herald*—Gray's Point, in memory of Lt. Andrew B. Gray, one of the first to suggest putting San Diego where it is now.

In the late 1860s, the almost simultaneous laying out of present-day San Diego by Alonzo Horton, and of National City, four miles up the bay, by Frank Kimball and his brother Warren, brought a need for adequate wharves. By the early autumn of 1868, a fine little wharf race was going on; Horton was building out, southwesterly, from the foot of Fifth Street and had passed the 500-foot mark, while S. S. Culverwell, another developer, was building west from about the foot of F Street. In 1871 the Kimballs finished

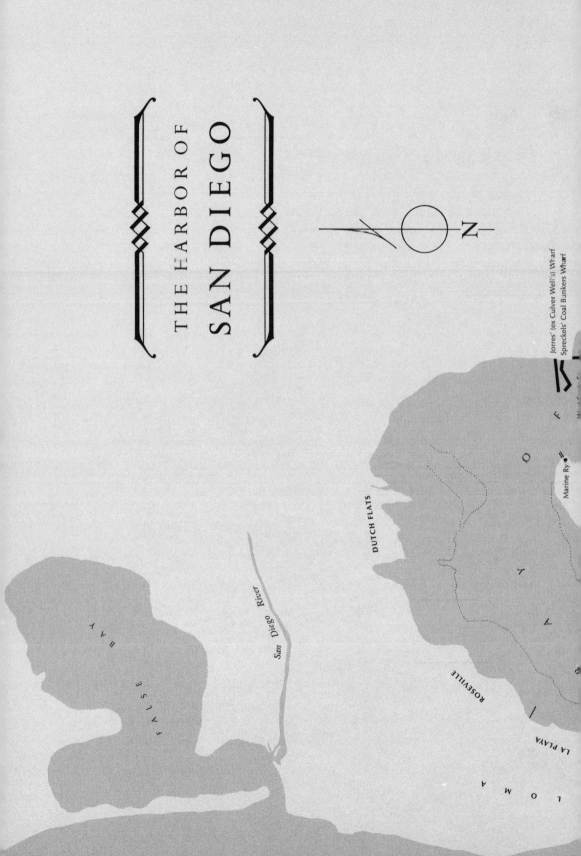

THE HARBOR OF
SAN DIEGO

N

Jorres' (ex Culver Well's) Wharf
Spreckels' Coal Bunkers Wharf

DUTCH FLATS

Marine Ry.

San Diego River

FALSE BAY

ROSEVILLE

LA PLAYA

LOMA

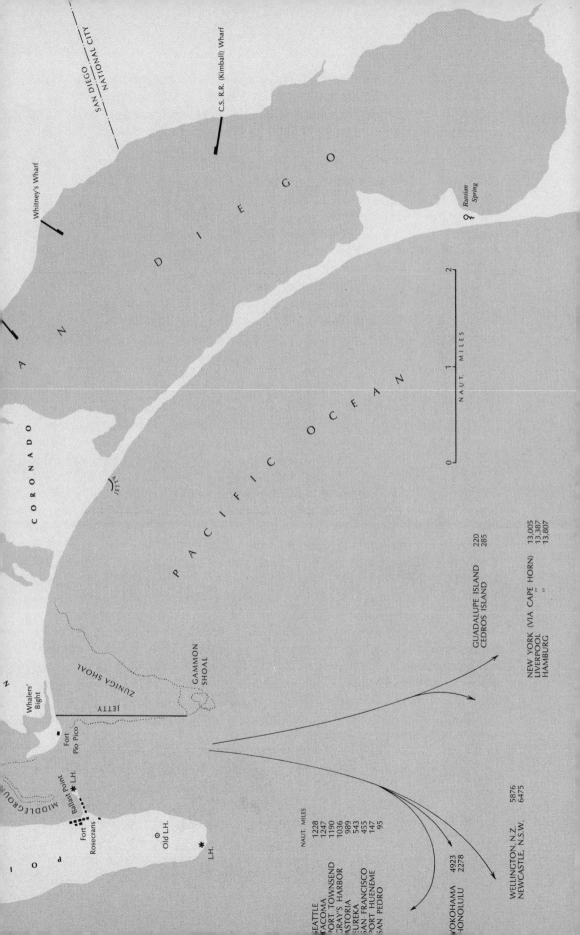

SAN DIEGO
NATIONAL CITY

C.S. R.R. (Kimball) Wharf

Whitney's Wharf

Russian
Spring

SAN DIEGO

CORONADO

2

NAUT. MILES

1

Whalers'
Bight

JETTY

PACIFIC OCEAN

GAMMON
SHOAL

ZUNIGA SHOAL

JETTY

Fort Pio Pico

0

MIDDLEGROUND

Ballast Point ★ L.H.

Fort
Rosecrans

Old L.H.

★ L.H.

	NAUT. MILES
SEATTLE	1228
TACOMA	1247
PORT TOWNSEND	1190
GRAY'S HARBOR	1036
ASTORIA	989
EUREKA	543
SAN FRANCISCO	455
PORT HUENEME	147
SAN PEDRO	95

GUADALUPE ISLAND	220
CEDROS ISLAND	285

NEW YORK (VIA CAPE HORN)	13,005
LIVERPOOL "	13,387
HAMBURG "	13,807

YOKOHAMA	4923
HONOLULU	2278

WELLINGTON, N.Z.	5876
NEWCASTLE, N.S.W.	6475

their wharf at National City; a few years later, with the coming of the California Southern Railroad, this wharf was considerably enlarged.

Pacific Mail, "opposition" coastwise steamers, and sailing vessels with everything from lumber to shoestrings and tin pans for San Diego, used both Horton's and Culverwell's wharves, while the Kimball wharf served the needs of National City both for long distance and inter-city waterborn cargo. Of the latter, there was quite a bit, the road between San Diego and National City being nothing about which to brag. Horton later sold his wharf to the Pacific Coast Steamship Co., who used it as a passenger/cargo terminal until shortly before the First World War, when they shifted their operations to the new Broadway Pier. Meanwhile William Jorres, a contractor who in 1872 built San Diego's original Court House, bought out Culverwell, and so what now was Jorres' Wharf became more important than it had been. Not only did Jorres handle ships' cargoes, but he supplied outward-bounders with such vital commodities as ballast and fresh water. He had a water-barge propelled by a single square sail, which was a familiar sight for many years, and he operated the little steam tug *Emma*.

In 1886 Elisha S. Babcock and Hampton L. Story, whose syndicate had bought and was developing the transbay peninsula of Coronado, started an ambitious wharf-building project on the site of Davis' ill-fated wharf of 1850. The Babcock & Story Wharf—really a system of wharves—consisted of a pier which was a continuation of Atlantic Street (now Pacific Highway) and terminated in the tiny slip for the Coronado Ferry Co.; angling away from it to the southeasterly was a massive timber pier with railroad tracks, right on the edge of the deepwater channel and capable of handling half a dozen big ships at once. Jutting out to the west was a smaller wharf with a white-washed building to serve as the U. S. Customs Service Barge Office, and near the center of this enclave they put up a rather story-book appearing two story, gray shingled building with a steep hip roof. When, a year or so later, they sold it to the Spreckels interests, this became the office of the Spreckels Brothers' Commercial Co., and the easterly and westerly arms of the wharf became the East Santa Fe and West Santa Fe Wharves. In the early 1890s a long red, corrugated-iron transit-shed was built on the easterly part to handle cargo for an ambitious but short-lived steamship operation handling inbound and outbound cargo between San Diego and the Orient—from which came its unofficial name of "Oriental Wharf". During the years when the American-Hawaiian Steamship Co. operated its "Tehuantepec Route" intercoastal freight service—from 1907 to 1914—they used it regularly. Its last service was right after the First World War, when the Navy brought many of the old "four-pipers" to the West Coast, and it became San Diego's first destroyer repair base.

Originally the big shipments of coal which came in for California Southern and for local consumption were merely dumped onto an open wharf like Kimball's or Babcock & Story's, to be shoveled up later into gondolas or dump-carts and hauled away. It was slow, messy and expensive, but it might have gone on indefinitely had not Babcock wanted to buy some cement from a San Francisco dealer. The merchant made it clear that he regarded San Diego as a jumping-off place, utterly lacking in substance or dependability, and that if Babcock wanted any cement he could jolly well come up to San Francisco and deal through a San Francisco broker. Having heard of John D. Spreckels, who had extensive shipping interests, Babcock telegraphed him; Spreckels was more obliging, and the cement was on its way at once.

The deal aroused Spreckels' curiosity. So he provisioned his yacht, a handsome two-masted schooner named *Lurline*, and sailed down to San Diego for a look around. Little did the natives realize, when the schooner came up into the wind and let go her anchor off the raw, new town, that she would change the course of local history. That was in the summer of 1887.

Spreckels liked what he saw, but there were flaws in the picture—and one of them was this silly business of dumping coal onto a wharf and then having to shovel it up again. He got together with his brother A. B. Spreckels, with Babcock and with Charles T. Hinde, who then was commercial agent for the Atchison, Topeka & Santa Fe Railway Co., and they formed the Spreckels Brothers' Commercial Company. Its purpose was to build a long wharf specifically for handling such cargoes as coal, cement, steel and other heavy bulk commodities. On Jan. 10, 1888, the first pile was driven for Spreckels' Wharf—or as it was more generally known, the Coal Bunkers. They already had a contract with the Santa Fe to handle the coal for all its locomotives in California.

On top of the long, heavily-built wharf was a bunker 645 feet long, divided into compartments 30 feet wide and 30 feet deep; it could hold 15,000 tons of coal at a time. At its westerly end an engine-house and boilers supplied power for the unloading machinery and for the cable-operated coal cars which ran on tracks on top of the bunkers, dumping their loads as they were required. Chutes and railroad tracks on each side of the bunkers made it possible to load two 20-car trains in a matter of minutes. The grim, black bulk of Coal Bunkers Wharf would be the bay's most prominent landmark from 1888 until it was torn down in the late 1920s. On its site today is Fishermen's Wharf at the foot of G St., while two blocks up that street is a sturdy brick building occupied by a dealer in surplus and general merchandise; it is the old Spreckels Brothers' warehouse.

When the boom broke and everyone got out who could, Spreckels hung on and even increased his holdings, which soon included the Coronado ferry, the Hotel del Coronado, two daily newspapers, downtown real estate, and the street-car system. For this he was roundly criticized, although it is difficult to argue that he didn't bail San Diego out when she was about to go down with all hands—and there was always a sizeable segment of the community which considered it *chic* to be a Spreckels-hater.

There were other wharves before steel and concrete and solid-fill piers took over, like the Russ Lumber Company's, and the West Coast Lumber Company's in shallow water along the Santa Fe tracks between First and State Streets; this area now is filled in. The San Diego Lumber Co. had one at the foot of Sixth; Benson's Wharf was built at the foot of Sigsbee in 1906 and McCormick's, a few blocks further south, in 1911. Standard Oil built beyond that, for its tankers, about the same time; Union Oil shared Benson's after moving from its modest tankage at the foot of Fourth, with a pipe-line which came in from the end of the Steamship Wharf a block away.

While a veritable armada of tall ships headed for San Diego from Swansea and Wellington and Hamburg and both Newcastles, that man-made marvel, Los Angeles Harbor, still was on the drawing-boards and San Diego was the seaport for most of Southern California. It is a bit droll to scan the pages of the *United States Coast Pilot* for as late as 1909 and read: "WILMINGTON . . . is of little commercial importance. There is a depth of 5 feet in the channel to the wharves . . . SAN PEDRO is the seaport for Los Angeles, about 21 miles inland. The depths alongside the wharves range from 20 to 24 feet . . . There is a large amount of domestic commerce in lumber, general merchandise, fish and dairy products, and the port has a rapidly increasing foreign commerce." By comparison it cites San Diego's wharfside depths of up to 28 feet and adds that "There is a large amount of foreign and domestic commerce . . . Lumber, iron, cement, guano and general merchandise are imported; fruit and dairy products are exported . . ."

In 1907 the channel across the bar at the entrance to San Diego Bay was dredged to 28 feet—it now is 42—and meanwhile Zuñiga Jetty, started in 1894, had been finished. It runs out 7,500 feet from the southwesterly tip of North Island, and protects the dredged channel from silting up.

Aids to navigation had not been lacking, even if, in the early days, Goodall, Nelson & Perkins, the steamship people, had to maintain the inside beacons themselves. The original Point Loma Lighthouse, atop the point, was lighted Nov. 15, 1855 and was soon found to be too high—an error which it took 36 years to rectify. "New" Point Loma Lighthouse, sometimes called "The Lower Light", was commissioned March 30, 1891; meanwhile Ballast Point Lighthouse had already been lit, on the night of Aug. 1, 1890.

Unlighted buoys were set, off the entrance, soon after California's first lighthouse tender, the *Shubrick*—which doubled as a revenue cutter—came out in 1858, and as late as February of 1873 she was still visiting San Diego with lighthouse supplies and to service the buoys. The first "sophisticated" aid was a whistle-buoy off Point Loma, set by the *Madrono* on Jan. 21, 1887. Just a year later it was moved to a point 3½ miles south of Ballast Point and its place was taken by a bell-buoy, both still in about the same positions, but lighted; there were no light buoys until well after the turn of the century.

That channel-deepening had been a long time coming. On Mar. 3, 1888, the Norwegian bark *Prince Edwards*, drawing 26 feet, had to anchor outside for three days, waiting for a high enough tide to let her cross the bar.

6. Elite of the Seven Seas

Though I tell many, there must still be others,
McVicar Marshall's ships and Fernie Brothers' . . .
— JOHN MASEFIELD

Despite a tendency by modern poets to abhor rhyme and meter, and to exalt the garbage-dump rather than the crashing breaker, there still are those who find peace and satisfaction in the works of an old master like Masefield. And in reading his verse, they will run across more than one ship which has towed in past Point Loma.

A lot of famous ships have made their landfall off Point Loma, and San Diego pilots have clambered up and over the rail to greet more than one master who left his name in the annals of the sea—men, for instance, like Brace-Winch Jarvis and Ninety-fathom Johnston and that delightful mariner-journalist Edward Payson Nichols, copies of whose little shipboard newspaper today are collectors' items.

First in the procession of ships-with-names probably was a rather pathetic little steamer called *Monumental City*, which wheezed slowly up to an anchorage off La Playa on May 27, 1852, with a tale of fever-stricken passengers, disabled machinery and, finally, fire at sea. Ten of her passengers had died and others had been left at Acapulco to (it was hoped) recover; it had taken her 25 days to make the 1450-odd miles from that Mexican port to San Diego. This, however, is not what made her famous—it is the fact that, a few months later, she became the first steamer to cross the Pacific.

"The *California*, huge, as slow as time . . ." the late Poet Laureate (who himself visited San Diego in the late 1920s) wrote in a masterpiece called, simply, *Ships*. And the *California*, a massive four-masted bark, came to San Diego in 1911, but with Wilson's house-flag hauled down and the merchant colors of Russia replacing the Red Duster. He goes on to mention "Stalwart *Drumcliff*, white-blocked, majestic *Sierras*"—and a pilot's battered log-book shows the *Sierra Ventana* here in 1896, *Sierra Estrella* in 1897 and *Sierra*

On the next page: "A forest of spars"—*trite, but it meant just that, in the winter of 1888, at Babcock & Storey's Wharf in San Diego. In the right foreground is the British bark* Trongate, *and just ahead of her is the swift Down Easter* Elwell. *The three-skys'l-yarder at the left is the Bath-built* Santa Clara, *later to join the fleet of the Alaska Packers Association, of San Francisco.*—HISTORICAL COLLECTION, TITLE INSURANCE & TRUST CO.

Blanca (she went missing in 1917) as a 1901 arrival. The German four-masted bark *Omega*, which called at San Diego in 1909, was the old *Drumcliff.* He speaks of the *Glaucus*, which tied up at Spreckels' Wharf in 1904, and of the "*Lochs, Counties, Shires, Drums,* the countless lines . . ." of which San Diego wharves served more than one— *County of Caithness, County of Pembroke, Fifeshire* and *Clackmannanshire* among them.

Too little has been told of the part which the Down Easters played in the building of the port—that is, with the exception of Richard Henry Dana, who had the good luck to get here during the Hispano-Mexican era and hence was deemed worthy of note by local historians. Forgotten are the names of the fine old *State of Maine,* the *Valley Forge,* the *Highland Light* and the *Benj. F. Packard*—to say nothing of the *Elwell,* the St. *Stephen,* the *Belvedere* and the *Tam O'Shanter.* All made San Diego between 1880 and 1905; so, to name a few others, did the *Santa Clara,* the *Bohemia* and that unfortunate example of America's attempt to build iron sailing vessels, the *T. F. Oakes.*

Captain Nichols, of the *Frank Pendleton,* carried with him a small printing-press and several fonts of type; on the long voyages, instead of writing letters to each of his many friends around Searsport, Me., he set up and printed *The Ocean Chronicle.* And never did San Diego receive a better "press" than in his issue of Sept. 19, 1887, printed after reaching Port Townsend, Washington Territory, from San Diego.

"There is one thing about San Diego as a port for shipping," he wrote, in part, "they do not try to squeeze money out of ships . . . we never did business with more agreeable people . . ." Less favorable was his view of a Latin American port visited on a prior voyage; his far-from-enthusiastic observations wound up with "The inhabitants are composed chiefly of men, women, and Custom House officers."

The story of the capsizing at San Francisco of the four-masted bark *Earl of Dalhousie,* and her rather spectacular salvaging and repair under the guidance of Capt. J. C. B. Jarvis, was still fresh in people's minds when Captain Jarvis brought his re-rigged ship in to San Diego in 1887, two years after the accident. A man of mechanical as well as nautical skill, he was the inventor of the mechanical brace-winch, which enabled a smaller crew to handle a ship with greater safety and speed than before, and was adopted on a world-wide basis; from then on he was known (and respectfully) as Brace-Winch Jarvis. Later he brought his family from Scotland to America and a son, Andrew Baxter Jarvis, after serving with the United States Navy in the First World War, settled at Alpine, in the foothills behind San Diego. He died August 24, 1966, and is buried at Fort Rosecrans National Cemetery, overlooking the bay into which his father, without help from tugs, had sailed the *Earl of Dalhousie* seventy-nine years before.

Perhaps even better known was the *Belted Will,* a famous British tea-clipper of 1866—but when she came to San Diego on July 4, 1889, she had been cut down to a bark rig, she was under the Swedish flag, and instead of tea her hold was full of coal. It had taken her 82 days from Australia, which was no flash passage, and so little notice was taken of her that when she left, 20 days later, no one even bothered to jot down her destination. A little higher in the social scale than a coal-drogher was the slim-hulled iron clipper *Miltiades* of wool-trade fame, and which once had carried a load of 470 emigrants out to New Zealand. When she came in to San Diego in 1887 it was with a full cargo of glass from Antwerp, largely for Los Angeles merchants; San Diego, in those days, was still the only sheltered port south of San Francisco.

The famous *Dalgonar*—huge for a three-masted ship, at 2,565 tons—brought in her cargo of coal from Newcastle, N.S.W., in 1892, on her first round-the-world voyage. Eleven years later she was in the news when the French four-masted bark *Loire*, in a living gale, took off all but three of her crew, shifting ballast having disabled her; the three victims, including her master, had been killed trying to get boats away. A derelict, the big ship drifted on for 5,000 miles, finally piling up in the Society Islands. Also visiting in 1892 was the handsome four-masted bark *Pass of Melfort*, and some old-timers called her fairest ship ever to visit the port. She called again in 1902, and San Diego saw her no more; on Christmas night of 1905 she went ashore at the entrance to Barclay Sound, British Columbia, and there were no survivors.

The Blue Ensign of the Royal Naval Reserve was flapping proudly from her gaff when the British ship *MacMillan* paid her first visit to San Diego on Sept. 28, 1881, bringing railroad iron from Antwerp; a few days later Capt. Charles Grey, resplendent in his Reserve uniform, greeted the guests at a shipboard reception attended by the Collector of Customs and other local bigwigs. She was in port for two months, discharging rails and loading wheat, and that gave time for another reception. This time the master, who was something of a musician and composer, entertained the ladies of the select Amphion Club—and in San Diego for more than half a century, the Amphion Club loomed large on the social calendar. The *MacMillan* called again, with less fanfare, in 1888 and in 1892.

In *Vignettes of the Sea*, the late Capt. Felix Riesenberg devoted a whole chapter to "The Bloody *Gatherer*"—and he mentioned too, among the blood-ships, the *Hecla*. Both were here in the elegant eighties and so was the *Gatherer's* fleet-mate *Harvester*, which had her own share of sailor trouble.

Sixty years later Don Stewart, he of the diamond-point memory, was to recall his slight bewilderment in 1907 when he rented a wherry to row out and around a handsome four-masted bark anchored in the stream; the name painted on her stern was *Manga Reva*, but the letters incised in the sides of her teakwood wheel-box said *Pyrenees*. And how right he was; the story of the salvage of the *Pyrenees* from Manga Reva Reef is a classic in the lore of man's endless conflict with the sea.

7. Sailor Trouble

A sailorman—said the night-watchman musingly—a
sailorman is like a fish, he's safest when 'e is at sea.

—W. W. JACOBS

Somewhere along the line a mate named José probably laid out a sailor named Pedro with the Spanish equivalent of a belaying-pin, while anchored in pre-Yankee San Diego Bay, but what appears to be the first account of a fair little mutiny had to do with the American whaler *Ocean* in 1847, as that staunch and smelly vessel lay off La Playa.

What sparked this small unpleasantness is not a matter of record, but the ensuing action was swift and to the point. The captain and the mates, each with a pistol stuck in the waistband of his pantaloons, waded in when the crew refused duty—one officer, meanwhile, having delayed long enough to run up a signal of distress. Of course, in 1847 San Diego had neither Coast Guard nor Harbor Police, but she had Philip Crossthwaite, himself an alumnus of Cape Horn, and a lot of rugged veterans of the Mormon Battalion who, having walked all the way to San Diego from Council Bluffs, Iowa, were in pretty fair shape. They rowed out to the *Ocean*, hoping for a bit of action, but were disappointed; it was all over and a complacent captain, puffing away on a stogie, leaned over the rail and thanked them anyhow. It seems that he and the mates had overpowered the leading fo'csl barrister, triced him up to the lanyards of the main rigging and worked him over with a cat-o-nine-tails. The crew got the message, and turned-to.

It would be far from the truth, however, to say that the *Ocean* affair was San Diego's last case of sailor trouble; there would be more of it, afloat and ashore, with the peak coming at the time of the boom of the late Eighties. There would be rough-stuff afloat and ashore, with gunplay, kidnapings—and even one bizarre case in which American Bluejackets came to the aid of some apprentices from a British windjammer, who had engaged the local police in a free-for-all.

Few masters had any more crew trouble than Capt. Charles Schnauer of the American ship *Harvester* back in 1888 when, in addition to protesting real or fancied grievances, whole crews would walk off just for the hell of it—and then seek re-employment at sharply increased rates. Sailors who signed on at San Diego demanded $50 a month instead of the going rate of $40, so Schnauer made a deal with someone in San Francisco to send him a non-union crew. Word of it leaked out, and the train in which they were riding to San Diego was intercepted at Oceanside, about 40 miles north, by as tough a mob of "loyal unionists" as you'd not care to meet in some dark alley. The recruits were "induced" to leave the train and the *Harvester* was still without a crew. Rail transportation having proven impractical, Schnauer had his next bunch of $40-a-monthers sent down in the steamer *City of Topeka*.

When the "Tapioca", as they used to call her, came in, the men were transferred to the tug *Gen. McPherson*, to be taken out to the anchored *Harvester*, but again the word had leaked. Tug and ship were surrounded by Whitehalls and skiffs and wherries loaded with unionists, and although they had been paid a month's wages in advance, the new men returned to the beach. That night most of the advance-money went across the bars in San Diego and there was general rejoicing at the discomfiture of Schnauer and his deserted ship, anchored far down the bay off La Playa. But while sailors and union officials frolicked, Schnauer was at work: A British vessel, the bark *Argo*, had arrived, with a crew getting probably not more than $10 a month. A couple of mornings later, union officials were quite upset to see the *Harvester* towing out to sea—and with obviously capable men aloft, loosing her sails. But if you think that they felt badly about it, how do you think the master and mates of the *Argo* felt when they found that they had an empty foc'sl?

While returning to his ship one dark night in 1887, the steward of the *Miltiades* was spotted by a union "enforcement squad" and was mistaken for an individual noted for his un-union thinking. A shot was fired and the steward went down, with a bullet through one leg—but when they saw their mistake, his attackers did the decent thing. They picked him up, carried him to the nearest saloon, bandaged his leg—and then poured so much red-eye into him that when, half an hour later, they deposited him on the *Miltiades'* deck, he was quite definitely feeling no pain.

Things were about at their worst late in 1887, and on the night of Nov. 7 of that year occurred what came to be known as "The *Darra* Outrage"—an incident which led directly to a cessation of the worst of the strong-arm stuff. The *Darra* was a British bark commanded by Capt. Robert Story; she had discharged cargo and hauled out into the stream, ready for sea, when she was approached in the darkness by two boat-loads of men who had learned that she had three non-union sailors aboard. The men in the boats, union officials and sympathizers, swarmed aboard fore and aft, and demanded that the three offending men be turned over to them. Captain Story refused and drew a revolver, but he was overpowered, the gun was wrenched from his hand, and while he and the two mates were cowed by one boatload of men, the others removed the men from the foc'sl and dragged them into the boats and ashore.

It now developed that the three men were British subjects—and as of 1887, England frowned upon this sort of thing. A complaint was lodged with the

Each assuming what he feels is a photogenic pose, officers and men of the British ship Isle of Arran, *just in from Newcastle, N.S.W., in the autumn of 1894, line up for a picture. One of Andrew Weir's ships, she lasted until Feb. 2, 1917, when a German submarine got her, 100 miles south of Kinsale.*—HISTORICAL COLLECTION, TITLE INSURANCE & TRUST CO.

British consul, and within hours the rumor was spreading that one of Her Majesty's men-o-war was on its way to San Diego, to protect the lives and property of British subjects. It may or may not have been so, but it worked; the three men were released, and waterfront violence went into something of a decline.

In those days San Diego had 64 grocery stores and 71 saloons, which more or less gives you the picture. Stingaree (sometimes called Stingaree Town) was the city's tawdry and unkempt counterpart of San Francisco's famous Barbary Coast—and after dusk, it was an excellent place to avoid. It abounded in dives and "dance-halls" and Chinese opium-dens, and a local newspaper sadly observed that after dark, ". . . a man cannot walk along the streets, minding his own business, without being hallooed at by the shameless women." It was the recreational area for the Cape Horn sailor, the man-o-warsman, the railroad boomer, the cow-poke and the amateur Paul Bunyans of the lumber-schooners; a few were well-behaved, but many were not.

One source of serious trouble was the attempt by local officialdom to balance a shaky municipal budget by reducing the already too small Police Department from 25 to 15 men. Some genius came up with the idea of substituting special deputy constables for the regular, paid policemen; the constables were willing to "live on pickings", as the saying went—collecting fees for serving subpoenas and attachments, and for turning in Navy deserters. To put the policing of "Sailor Town" in the hands of a crowd of fee-hungry amateurs with clubs was, as they should have known, just asking for trouble— and trouble they got. In one general fracas which ensued, a sailor from the U. S. S. *Charleston* was so badly beaten that he crawled off into the hay-loft of a nearby livery stable, where he died. Now groups of angry bluejackets began to range the streets, and "the law" went into hiding until the *Charleston* sailed.

Years later—sailors have long memories—the trouble boiled up again, even though the "specials" had long since been replaced by regular, if untrained, police. On the night of Nov. 6, 1902, a couple of frisky apprentices from the *Pass of Melfort* tangled with the lawmen in Stingaree and were about to be hauled off to jail when their predicament was observed by a group of sailors from the old U. S. S. *Boston*—a ship herself noted, on occasion, for turning certain parts of San Diego into disaster areas. What if the apprentices were from a British ship? They were brother mariners—and with a shout of "Remember the *Charleston!*" the *Boston's* men moved in. With great difficulty the police got the two youngsters to jail, and within minutes the jail was surrounded by a mob of American bluejackets. They dispersed only when the apprentices (one with a bandaged scalp) were released.

San Diego can claim, although a bit vicariously, some of the credit for cleaning up unspeakable conditions in the American merchant marine and ending the gory day of the bucko mate, with his belaying pin and his brass knuckles—although we should remember that the problems of that some-times unjustly maligned individual were, at times, pretty hairy; it's no fun getting a ship to sea with a crew well larded with drunks, incompetents and trouble-makers. San Diego's part in this social reform stems from the arrival of the British bark *Glamis* in 1890. Among the members of her crew who went over the side one dark night was a tough and articulate young Scotsman named Walter MacArthur.

It didn't take much subsequent time in American ships to show him that there was a need for straightening things out, so far as the lot of the American seaman was concerned. He joined the old Coast Seamen's Union, became its secretary and the right-hand man of the crusading Andrew Furuseth, and was the author of a little paperback called *The Red Record;* it was a grisly chronicle, from official records, of some outstanding cases of brutality to seamen. For instance: "HENRY B. HYDE ... First mate of the ship charged with breaking a seaman's wrist with a belaying pin and otherwise ill-treating him. Case dismissed on ground of 'justifiable discipline' ... I. F. CHAP-MAN ... Carpenter was ironed hand and foot and triced up to the spanker-boom for an hour ... [the captain] acquitted by the Commissioner on the ground that the punishment was 'not very cruel'."

Later *The Red Record* was reprinted serially in *The Coast Seamen's Journal* and did much to bring about some badly needed legislation. MacArthur, who later himself became U. S. Shipping Commissioner at San Francisco, was the author a few years before his death of a gold-mine of information for windjammer historians—*Last Days of Sail on the West Coast.*

The last real mutiny was, appropriately, aboard the last Cape Horner to make San Diego—the British full-rigged ship *Dudhope,* Capt. Francis Hodgins. She arrived Nov. 30, 1914, to discover that since she left Hamburg on July 12, the First World War had broken out. Actually, her master and first mate knew it; off the coast of South America one evening an unidentified British tramp steamer had signalled her with a Berwick lamp: "ENGLAND AND GERMANY AT WAR CAUTION". Luckily, only those two officers could read and understand the message. They were, of course, British—but the second mate and most of the crew were German, and she could easily have wound up as another *Seeadler.*

At San Diego the crew accepted the news stoically, but just the same, one of them got ashore and found a lawyer. The next day papers were served, alleging that war had cancelled the contract; the ship was libelled, and pay-off was demanded. Just before dawn of Dec. 11 all hands were called aft and the articles were read to them. Seven refused duty and were promptly ironed and herded into the foc's'l; the tug which had been standing by came alongside on signal, and the *Dudhope* was on her way.

But she was not long for this world. She got to Portland, loaded grain for the U.K. and headed back for home. They say she was only about 200 miles from Queenstown when a German submarine got her.

8. At the End of a Long, Stout Hawser

Shorn of the beauty of her white wings, she wound obediently after the tug through the maze of invisible channels.

—JOSEPH CONRAD

Ferryboats have their dedicated and at times vociferous afficionados, which is entirely proper. There is something about the pilot-schooner, footing silently through the fog, which catches the imagination, and there are those who sing the well-deserved praise of the fire-boat, the police launch—and the Coast Guard cutter smashing out into the teeth of a gale in accordance with that rugged service's unofficial motto: "You've got to go out—whether you come back or not!" And let us not overlook the tug-boats as they churn up and down the harbors at their daily tasks, or make suicidal forays into white water where a freighter hangs on a pinnacle rock and a million dollars in insurance hangs in the balance.

Up to 1881 San Diego was innocent of tugs. Masters of schooners and of infrequent square-riggers got into port by their own skill and the backbreaking toil of their crews at the sheets and braces. Coming in wasn't so bad; with the normal prevailing northwesterly wind they got up as far as La Playa close-hauled on the port tack. Then they could ease off and go booming up the bay, all the way to National City if they were of a mind to. Getting out was something else again—a maddening series of short tacks—and it is small wonder that captains frequently arranged it so that they would be departing on the same day that some coasting steamer was leaving. For a few dollars the paddler *Orizaba* or the "hog boat" *Bonita* or even the little Mexican steamer *Carlos Pacheco*, outward bound, would pass them a line, and away they'd go.

When California Southern began its track-laying in 1881 and ordered several shiploads of rails via Cape Horn, they decided that a tug was needed and bought the tiny *Rover* in San Francisco. She was all ready when their

At the end of the Bahada's *towline, the three-masted schooner* Wawona *leaves San Diego astern, in 1912.*—PHOTO BY AUTHOR

first load of rails arrived in the *Trafalgar* on Aug. 7—but the big Cape Horner simply ignored her and sailed on, up to National City. However, she did local towing for a decade—even though, on one occasion, the sidewheel ferryboat *Coronado* had to come to her aid when she was trying to buck a strong ebb tide, with the *Wilna* in tow. In 1891 she was sold and her engine and boiler were taken out, and she went to Hilo, Hawaii, as a two-masted schooner.

She was not alone in coming to San Diego as a steamer and leaving as a windjammer. A small Army steamer, the *Gen. McPherson*, built at San Francisco in 1867, was bought by Babcock & Story and came to San Diego early in 1887. A comfortable passenger cabin in the after end of her deck-house made her useful as an excursion-boat as well, and she used to take fishing parties to the Coronado Islands—especially after the boom flattened and, with the *Santa Fe* in service, she became, as the British say, redundant. A few years later they removed her superstructure and machinery and she became a trading-schooner, running as far south as Guaymas. Sold to a Portland operator she sailed up to the Columbia and, eventually, Alaska in 1898.

Next after the Rover came the *Emma*, built originally as a yacht or excursion-boat in 1881. Gus Jorres, son of the wharf-owner, had her for a number of years and her varied tasks included the noisesome one of towing the garbage-scow *Utilissimo* out to sea and back; she was dismantled in 1901. Meanwhile, in 1888, had come Spreckels' twin-screw tug *Santa Fe*. For some unknown reason no one ever called her "the tug *Santa Fe*", but followed the phraseology of the days of "the *Dreadnaught* packet" and "the *Nancy* brig". She was always referred to as "the *Santa Fe* tug".

If the names of all the ships whose hawsers she has boarded off Point Loma were to be written down, it would read like a *Who's Who* of the sea. And she did her work faithfully—although, tugs being only human, there were days when she couldn't win. There was, for instance, that embarrassing incident when she got too close to the schooner *F. S. Redfield* while attempting to tow her in, and was "de-smokestacked" by the *Redfield's* jibboom. Quickly the schooner made sail again and the *Santa Fe*, her boiler now unusable, suffered the ignominy of being towed home by the vessel she was supposed to be towing. And Capt. Fred Klebingat—at that time donkeyman in the barkentine *S. N. Castle*, up from the Tuamotos in 1911— recalls sighting her some miles away, and taking in their sails. To their surprise the tug hove-to while still about two miles off, so they made sail again and stood over toward her. Then it was explained: the tug had plenty of coal but she was not equipped with a condenser. That was as far out as she dared to go with her limited supply of boiler-feed water, and still be sure of having enough to get her home.

In 1902 Spreckels Brothers brought the fine little steam tug *Bahada*— built by Moran of Seattle—down to San Diego, and the faithful *Santa Fe* was relegated to relief status, finally being converted into a water-barge about the time of the First World War. The steel-hulled *Bahada* took over what was left of the dwindling windjammers, did general harbor towing and, on occasion, doubled as a water-barge; she had tankage for 13,000 gallons of potable water. She also, of course, had the job of acting as a "rudder" for the huge log-rafts, entering port after the long tow down from the Columbia.

By the outbreak of the First World War the windships were gone and the *Bahada* was losing money. She was sold to the Hercules Powder Co., which had a war-time plant at Chula Vista, on the upper bay; they converted her into an oil-burner and used her for towing kelp-barges. Then she went to San Pedro where, in 1923, she was in a collision with the tanker *Richmond*, resulting in one death. Finally returning to her native Puget Sound, she went down with all hands, off Huckleberry Island, some time during the night of Nov. 21, 1926.

Now, with the exception of a few "gas boats" of 75-horsepower or so, San Diego was without a tug until the 1920s, when the handsome Diesel tug *Palomar* was built for Star & Crescent Boat Co.; shortly afterward they converted the motorship *Bergen* (originally the little steamer *Sue H. Elmore*, of Tillamook, Ore.) into the tug *Cuyamaca*. Later would come their Diesel-electric *Challenger* and the big, steel *Starcrescent*, built for long-distance towing, in the barge field. In the interim the Navy would step in with a tug, for free, when a log-raft or a big liner needed help. To have sent in a bill would have been illegal competition with "free enterprise"—but by tradition, the officer in command of the tug which docked and undocked a Panama Pacific liner was not supposed to be surprised if he found, in his parked car, a fifth of Scotch, Prohibition or not.

Offshore towing in and out of San Diego—and mostly in—brought the big ones, and not the least of them was Spreckels' tug *Fearless*, which came down from San Francisco early in 1892 to tow home the disabled steamer *Sirius*. Intimates of John D. Spreckels always claimed that he was, at heart, just a frustrated sea-captain, happier by far in a "working" vessel than in a yacht. And this was borne out by the *Fearless*, which had a posh "owner's stateroom" and guest staterooms for eight; it wasn't until years later that he bought a steam yacht. During the Spanish-American War the *Fearless* was taken up by the Navy; many times later she was back in San Diego as the U. S. S. *Iroquois*, and she served the Navy for years.

To replace the *Fearless* they brought the *L. Luckenbach* out from the East Coast and re-named her *Defiance*, but even before her name was changed she visited San Diego. Early in December of 1900 she came in to top off with coal and provisions before heading for Santa Rosalia, Baja California, and she returned on Feb. 2, 1901, with the battered and leaking *Edmund* in tow. The *Edmund*, a German four-masted bark, had got onto the beach while leaving the Mexican port and her rescue, after being pumped out nine times, still is one of the epics of West Coast salvage. In later years the *Defiance* was an occasional visitor, towing Standard Oil barges from the northern refineries. And it was she that towed the French ship *Daniel* from San Diego to the Columbia late in 1902, so that she could meet a dead-line and not lose a charter to load grain for Europe. In another speed-up move many years before—this was in 1887—the ship *Highland Light* was sailing down to San Diego with a load of badly needed coal; so critical was the local fuel situation that the Spreckels tug *Relief* was sent out from San Francisco, intercepted her off the Farallones and yanked her on to San Diego just in time to avert a genuine coal-famine. That same year, the schooner *Nora Harkins* made several trips from Fort Bragg to San Diego in tow of the original tug *Sea Lion,* bringing redwood for the booming, lumber-hungry town.

In the annals of San Diego's offshore towing, however, the first name you will hear from old-timers is Benson—and indeed the Benson Lumber Co. of San Diego wrote a unique page in West Coast towing with their huge log-rafts. It started when the Spreckels tug *Dauntless* brought the first log-raft in from the Columbia, some 1,000 miles away, on Sept. 7, 1906, and lasted until 1941, with from one to five of the huge rafts coming in each summer.

The first raft was 600 feet long and 44 feet wide, cigar-shaped and containing 4,000,000 board-feet of lumber held together by 110 tons of stud-link chain, and it took the *Dauntless* an even fortnight to make it. Later the rafts would go to 900 feet long and 6,000,000 board-feet—and there were times when bad weather would pull the passage-time out to three weeks.

During the Second World War, of course, log-rafting would have been out of the question, what with Japanese submarines on the prowl. A torpedo into a raft wouldn't have done it too much harm, but it would have knocked loose a lot of saw-logs—and all you need, during a war, is an ocean full of big, floating logs. The last raft, oddly enough, caught fire off Santa Cruz in the early autumn of 1941. What with lowering war-clouds, years of opposition to the rafts by shippers and by seafaring unions and other real or fancied objections, there was a certain amount of eyebrow-raising when a young lieutenant from the Fire Marshall's office in San Diego boarded the damaged raft, and reported a definite odor of phosphorous.

So the rafts are gone and so are the tugs which towed them—the *Dauntless, Hercules, Humaconna, Sea Scout* and second *Sea Lion.* The roster is impressive, especially when you add those other off-shore tugs—like the famous old *Richard Holyoke,* which came down in 1880 to tow the disabled Mexican gunboat *Mexico* up to San Francisco for repairs.

And in all those long tows down from the Columbia, there was very little trouble. However, Capt. A. F. Raynaud, Seattle marine surveyor, recalls a painful incident right in San Diego Bay when, half a century ago, he was serving in the *Sea Rover.* He recalls that as they were passing Ballast Point the mate, for some unknown reason, decided to pay out a few fathoms of wire from the towing-winch. With the strain at its forward end relaxed, the huge raft took a sheer and poked its nose into the mud; the tide carried the other end around, and they had the channel effectively blocked. This bottled up a couple of passenger steamers and some Navy ships, and made everyone very unhappy. Freeing the 900-foot raft was, of course, far beyond the combined strength of the *Sea Rover* and the *Bahada*—as was pointed out to the Senior Officer Present when he ordered the obstruction removed forthwith. Taking the hint, the S. O. P. sent Navy tugs to help, and the cork to San Diego Bay was pulled.

In the secrecy which then covered ships' movements there called at San Diego, as the Second World War was ending, one of the last commercial steam tugs which it is likely that the port will ever see. The name was *Storm King* and her master was a Captain Carl Carrillo, of that famous family of Spanish-Californian pioneers.

Those were fitting names on which to close the book.

9. Meanwhile, with adze and Beetle . . .

And now throughout the shipyard's bounds
Were heard the intermingled sounds
Of axes and of mallets plied
With vigorous strokes on every side.

—HENRY WADSWORTH LONGFELLOW

If anyone wanted to take the trouble of wading through a lot of musty archives in Madrid, he might come up with the name of San Diego's first boatbuilder and the name of the boat—for, being Spanish, she certainly had one. Anyway, the year was 1804, the vessel was a flat-boat about 25 feet long, she was used for the logistical support of Fort Guijarros on Ballast Point— and she lasted until 1827. By this time the Spanish garrison had become the Mexican garrison and when she was wrecked at a place vaguely described as "Los Adobes" they broke her up and used the lumber for a wharf.

The next boatbuilder of record was Capt. James Keating, lighthouse-keeper at Point Loma, who appears to have had a bit of time on his hands. In 1857 he built a schooner named *Loma* which, according to Editor John Judson Ames of the *Herald,* was launched and christened ". . . in due and ancient form." And why couldn't he have told us more about her? Tonnage? Dimensions? Was she built at La Playa or at Ballast Point, or on the beach over at New Town? For shame, John Judson Ames!

Along Atlantic Street were the modest boat-shops, where you would run onto such good old Down East names as Enos Wall and Amos Pettingill and Franklin Gregory. Joseph Supple came out from New York in 1886, built the scow-schooner *Utilissimo* and the little steamer *Roseville,* speculated in real estate—and lost his shirt when the boom collapsed in 1889. So he packed up his adze and his broad-axe and his caulking-beetles and his wooden planes and moved to Portland, Ore. He started all over, and with better luck this time; among other things he turned out nine river steamers for the Yukon and several for the Columbia, and during the First World War he built eleven ocean-going freighters for the U. S. Shipping Board.

John Nation, about whom too little is known, made local boatbuilding history on Dec. 19, 1881, when he launched the little excursion-boat *Emma,* the first steam vessel built in San Diego. She was only 51.5 feet long and grossed a modest 18 tons—but you have to start somewhere. She was built on the beach near the Army barracks, and after he sold her to Gus Jorres two years later, he vanished from the local record.

Soon afterward Christian Telson arrived from Evansville, Ind.—and there was a shipbuilder with a real story. As a young man he had worked in the Navy Yard at Charleston, S.C., his last job there being to help scuttle the U. S. S. *Merrimac*, lest she fall into enemy hands. A few hours later the Confederates over-ran the place and Telson became a prisoner of war. He was promptly put to work, with others, raising the sunken war-vessel and converting her into the C.S.S. *Virginia*, the history-making ironclad which soon after slugged it out with the U. S. S. *Monitor*. At San Diego Telson built the 528-ton ferryboat *Silver Gate*, the West Coast's first propeller-driven double-end ferry, and the largest vessel to be built in San Diego until more than thirty years later; she was launched Nov. 15, 1887. He also built "the *Santa Fe* tug" of fond memory, and wound up years later in a modest shop on Columbia Street, turning out huge skiffs for the fishermen.

In the early 1890s Jerry Nichols (his real name was Jireh) came to San Diego from Benicia, Calif., where he had worked with Matthew Turner, one of the West's most famous shipbuilders. He bought the shop of George E. P. Hunt, who also ran a bath-house (the waters of San Diego Bay were crystal-clear in those days) and turned out some famous yachts.

Around the turn of the century Manuel Goularte, a Portuguese boatbuilder of uncommon skill, started a shop near the foot of Fifth Street and hired as an apprentice a young man named Manuel Madruga, whose family had pioneered the Portuguese colony on Point Loma in 1876. In later years Madruga would achieve fame as a designer of big tunaboats, and superintendent of their construction.

The Campbell brothers, David and George, ran a modest advertisement in 1908: "General machine work—Autos stored and repaired—Steam, gas and marine work." They had the agency for Pope Hartford and Stevens Duryea cars, then climbed the social ladder to take over sales and service for Pierce-Arrows and Marmons—and then gradually dropped automobiles to go exclusively and successfully into shipbuilding, under their original name of the Campbell Machine Co.

Joe Fellows, noted boatbuilder in the Los Angeles area, opened a plant at the foot of Hawthorn Street around 1911; Clem Stose was in charge. Four years later, when the area was filled in during San Diego's first major port development, the plant was moved to the foot of Sampson Street and became the San Diego Marine Construction Co., later taken over by Capt. O. J. Hall of the Star & Crescent Boat Co. and other enterprises.

Now the clouds of the First World War were lowering, and San Diego would see its first wartime shipyard, as well as its first steamers built since the 1880s. At the foot of Thirty-second Street the Pacific Marine & Construction Co. set up a shipyard under contract with the U. S. Shipping Board,

About where the County Administration Center stands today, A. R. Robbins was repairing boats, and manufacturing marine gasoline engines, when this view was taken early in 1914; at the left they are working on the concrete bulkhead of the Embarcadero, San Diego's first major port improvement. Other marine engines built in San Diego, but in even more modest numbers, were the Hensley and the Baker.—HISTORICAL COLLECTION TITLE INSURANCE & TRUST CO.

and began building two concrete-hulled tankers, the *Cuyamaca* and the *San Pasqual*. And for cement ships, they weren't at all bad-looking; they had fantail sterns, engines amidships, two masts and the same type of "capped" stacks which, in the next World War, would distinguish some 2,700 Liberty Ships. They were of 6,486 gross tons, on dimensions of 420.7 x 54.0 x 34.3, and were powered by reciprocating engines of 2,800 horsepower. Although meant for wartime use, they weren't finished until 1920 and their careers were brief; by then, even conventional steel ships were a drug on the market. However, the yard provided San Diego with an outstanding fringe benefit: the nucleus of today's Naval Station, the former Destroyer Base.

Again the construction of steamers died out and San Diego went back to building fishing vessels—but now the modest fish-boat was a deep-sea job, eventually ranging as far afield as South America. From Campbell, San Diego Marine, Rask's and a few smaller yards, the bigger and bigger tuna-boats were being launched. Steam would not return until the Second World War when a new yard, the Lynch Shipbuilding Co., turned out several big steam tugs for the Navy.

Today Lynch's is gone—and on the site is the sprawling 80 acres of the National Steel & Shipbuilding Co., which had built 50 refrigerator barges for the Navy and three big floating cranes for the Army Transportation Corps. Now they brought out a modest 52-foot class of tunaboats, quickly went into bigger ones, and to show that they were versatile turned out the marine laboratory-ship *Velero IV*, for the University of Southern California. Tunaboat building continued, but the Korean war brought orders for tugs and minesweepers and cargo-barges. And in the late 1950s someone thought that it might be a good idea to get into the "big ship" game. They built an experimental ship for the Army and an oceanographic ship for the U. S. Coast & Geodetic Survey—and then came a small deluge of both conventional and "engines aft" C-3 cargo vessels of 17,000 tons, and 22,000-ton C-4s, each carrying a dozen passengers. Deliveries have been made to the American President Lines, States Steamship Co., American Mail Line and American Export-Isbrandtsen Lines. For the State of Washington they have built the four largest double-ended ferries in the world, 382-foot giants each capable of digesting 160 automobiles and 2,067 passengers—and ferrying them between Puget Sound ports at 20 knots. Sentimentally, however, they like to point to the new U. S. S. *San Diego*, scheduled for completion in 1969—which is San Diego's 200th anniversary year. She is one of four 581-foot AFSs, combat store ships which will be, in effect, gargantuan floating super-markets, carrying everything from food to electronic parts. Also under construction are seventeen of the big, new LSTs—tank landing ships—which are a far cry from the familiar "Large Slow Targets" of the Second World War.

Repair facilities, too have grown up through the years—up from the days when they used to beach schooners and small steamers at high tide, work on them when the water dropped, and then float them off when the tide came in again. Careening, that classic technic of Drake's time, apparently was little used in San Diego, although there is at least one case of a ship being "hove down" for scraping her copper. She was the little Tasmanian bark *J. L. Hall*, 682 tons, and the job was done at the north side of Spreckels' Wharf some time in December of 1894.

There were a few small marine railways, operated by hand-powered capstans, along the beach, but the first large repair facility was the one built by the San Diego Marine Railway & Drydock Co. at the northeast tip of North Island in the winter of 1887-88, and known throughout Southern California for many years simply as "The Marine Ways". It was the brain-child of Capt. William Bell, a boat-builder from Redwood City, and was financed by W. W. Stewart, then the city's leading commission merchant. A horizontal steam-engine, impressively geared down to the wildcat, worked the massive anchor-chain which hauled the cradle out of the water; first vessel to be docked there was the schooner *San Pedro*, on May 5, 1888. Soon after, the great boom collapsed, and Stewart was considering an offer to lease it to San Francisco interests when he learned that they were merely leasing outport shipyards and keeping them idle to remove competition; he angrily rejected the offer, and shortly afterward disposed of the installation to the Spreckels interests—which, like himself, refused to desert San Diego when her champagne days were over. The Spreckels operated the marine railway until the First World War, and its local clientele included the ferryboats, local tugs, and small Navy and Army steamers. From elsewhere came the San Pedro steamers *Hermosa* and *Warrior* and, among others, the barkentines *Modoc* and *S.N. Castle* and the four-masted schooners *Irene* and *Samar*. The steel-hulled topsail-schooner *Americana*, 959 gross tons and 204 feet long, is said to have been the largest one ever hauled there.

For many years North Island, now occupied by the Naval Air Station, was populated solely by some thousands of jackrabbits and by Old Cap'n Waters —Capt. Bob Waters, who ran the marine ways. And it was a voting precinct, in which Waters was both the election-board and the sole voter; each year the local press would solemnly announce that "North Island Goes 100% Republican". But that was not Old Cap'n Waters' only distinction: If a ship was being hauled out and some idiot had set a bilge-block improperly, or a steamer passed by and caused a swell which threatened to topple her over, he would display a grasp of the more robust part of the English language which could boil the pitch out of deck-seams. It was worth walking along miles of beach, or sculling yourself across the bay with one oar, just to hear him.

But now it's all over. There are big marine railways and floating drydocks all over the place, plus the huge graving-dock at the Naval Station. San Diego's most colorful and most single-minded voting precinct has faded into nostalgic memory.

10. Lance and Net and Hook

So we on with our coats and we manned the boats
For the point where the whale she blew.

—WALLACE IRWIN

In the first half of the Nineteenth Century, Yankee whalers were sparse and casual visitors to San Diego, and the local fishing industry was limited to those among the local *paisanos* who had enough ambition to bait a hook and toss it into the then clear and sparkling waters of the bay.

It never was a whaling port in the sense that locally-based whalemen would head for the high seas in barks or schooners, although from time to time a fair amount of oil was coopered at the modest local try-works, from whales caught close to shore. In the 1840s, female whales calved in San Diego Bay—a situation not overlooked by some of the transplanted New Englanders who made up the local seafaring population after the American occupation and who, by 1853, were taking advantage of it. Five years later there were two whaling companies located on Ballast Point, and when the wind was right it bore the robust effluvia from the bubbling try-pots and the partly processed carcasses, all the way to San Diego. In the 1870-71 season, the first one recorded with any accuracy, they produced nearly 22,000 gallons of oil; the next season, which was the best, showed 55,000 gallons of oil and 200 pounds of whalebone. By 1886 it was down to around 15,000 gallons and steadily declining.

In 1884 Capt. Enos Wall moved his whaling station from Ballast Point, across the channel to North Island, where there was a fresh-water spring and a little slough which came to be known as Whalers' Bight; it's all filled in now, and part of the Naval Air Station. Wall, whilom lighthouse-keeper, boat-builder and generally good man around the water, is said to have had the only whaling schooner to operate in local waters; that was the little *Sierra*, in 1883. However, two whalers did outfit from San Diego: Capt. Samuel Warren Hackett, who had started as a whaleman in New England at the age

---

Live or chopped bait, cast over the stern by the tuna-boat's "chummer", brings the fish to the surface; there they go crazy and will chomp down on one of the barbless hooks as quickly as on a live sardine. Here the action is lively as they hit a school of "one-pole" tuna—small enough to be handled by one man.—FRED REIF COLLECTION

of 16, outfitted the schooner *European* around the 1860s and went whaling down the Lower Coast, and in 1885 the San Francisco whaling schooner *Clara Light* provisioned at San Diego for a whaling cruise in the Okhotsk Sea.

As late as 1872, no less than fifteen whales were reported as seen inside of Ballast Point at one time; they say that it was the increasing number of steamers, in and out of the bay, which scared them off. The whalemen were still operating in boats from shore and, even in those days, used bomb lances—one of which blew up aboard the sloop *Newhope*, taking off most of a whaleman's hand.

Sealing also took the attention of San Diego mariners, and not merely for oil. More than 100 fur seal skins were brought in on Jan. 21, 1880, by the big sloop *Annie Heron*, from American waters; six months later the sloop *Isabella* arrived from the Lower Coast with 400 seal skins, a single elephant seal skin and 13 barrels of seal oil. Old timers recalled elephant seals on the Coronado Islands, in Mexican waters about 15 miles below San Diego, before unregulated sealing, chiefly for their oil, all but brought this interesting species to extinction. Just in the nick of time the Mexican government stepped in to protect the last herd, on Guadalupe Island, 220 miles to the south. By the mid-1920s this herd was down to about 125, but under protection it has increased encouragingly.

Capt. Joseph O'Cain must have overlooked a few sea-otters, because as late as the summer of 1880 the schooner *John Stillson* brought in, from Guadalupe, 200 fur seal skins and "several otters"; a few months before, the *Newhope* also had landed otter pelts in San Diego. Today it is a federal offense, with a stiff fine and prison sentence, for molesting any of the few living sea otters.

The first commercial fishermen included the local pilots, for there simply wasn't enough shipping to keep them busy, and frequently the local press would report that Capt. S. S. Dunnells or Capt. James Niles had, the previous day, brought in a fine catch of barracuda. Most of the fishermen were Down Easters, who deeply resented the influx of Chinese fishermen in the early 1880s.

For a number of years, Chinese junks were a common sight on San Diego Bay. Although of typically Oriental design they were locally built, of California redwood, the planks edge-nailed together with common black "cut" nails. They were fast and handy—so much so that both the Chinese and the junks' subsequent American owners found them quite well adapted to smuggling. A good deal of fish caught for the retail trade, including pompano and mullet, were netted right in the bay. Other fish, both for local use and for shipment to San Francisco, came in by the tiny schooners and big sloops of what was called "The Mosquito Fleet".

The Portuguese colony, later to play the leading part in San Diego fishing, started when Manuel Madruga arrived from the island of Pico, in the Azores, in 1876. Later Portuguese arrivals came either from overseas direct or via

Gloucester, Mass., or Half Moon Bay, Calif. The first fish-brokerage house was established in 1905 by Joe Lawrence and Manuel Soares.

Around the turn of the century, the first Italian fishermen arrived. Steve Ghio shows up in the 1901 City Directory and so does Bart Ghio, who had owned four prospering schooners out of Genoa—until a gale wiped out his whole fleet and he came to America for a fresh start. At first they used big flat-bottomed skiffs with oars and a single sail, and then the slim, double-ended "Columbia River salmon-boats"—the type actually originated on the Sacramento—which were flush-deck sloops with centerboards. The helmsman sat in a tiny hatch at the stern; just ahead of him was the main hatch, for the fish, and a smaller third hatch, just abaft the mast, led into a hold containing gear and a couple of crude bunks. There was a large influx of Italian fishermen from San Francisco following the big fire in 1906, and now more and more of the "Monterey boats" with their clipper bows and rounded sterns began to appear, as did the heavy-duty marine gasoline engine. The colorful day of sail was over.

Fish canning, which for a number of years was the city's principal industry, got away to a faltering start in 1909 when Edward Hume and A. J. Steele set up a small plant at La Playa, for canning sardines in olive oil. Two years later the Pacific Tuna Canning Co. started up at the foot of F Street; their plant burned down the following year, but was re-built at the foot of Twenty-sixth. Tuna had been canned at San Pedro in 1908, to receive a cool reception from the housewife—who in the world ever heard of tuna? In a few years, however, it was better known, and in 1912 the Premier Packing Co. opened a plant at the foot of Crosby St.; after numerous amalgamations it merged into the Van Camp Seafood Co. in 1923. The big Westgate plant, dating back to 1921, had been the Arrow Packing Corp. of 1918.

In the early days they canned nothing but albacore, which was—and to a limited extent still is—caught locally. This meant boats of modest size, say 40 or 45 feet long, which brought their catch in every day to fish-tender barges, bearing the flamboyant signs of the rival canneries to which they belonged.

Around 1916 it was discovered that the more plentiful bluefin tuna also could be canned, although this generally was done by packers in the Los Angeles area, and five years later they began to pack yellowfin tuna as well. This meant practically year-around fishing, and voyages farther and farther to sea by increasingly larger boats. Refrigerating machinery ceased to be a luxury, tunaboats became radio-equipped, and Guy Silva even introduced a small seaplane for fish-scouting. Cynics viewed this as a clear sign that Silva must be some kind of a nut, just as others clucked sadly and shook their heads when M. O. Medina, in 1926, built the "monstrous" tunaboat *Atlantic* —for who but a madman would build a fish-boat 110 feet long? In a few short years, she was dwarfed by the newer ones. Medina had been right, and so had Silva.

Japanese fishermen, moving in from San Pedro as the needs of the canneries grew, started to appear about 1917; they fished albacore during the summer, and when the season was over many of them found work on the truck-farms in the upper bay area. There was even a Japanese boat-builder, T. Iwata, who was kept busy for several years while the Japanese, like the others, graduated into bigger and bigger tunaboats.

The effect of the First World War on the fishing industry had been relatively slight; in 1941-45, however, this was far from the case. With enemy submarines actually operating in California waters, even fishing becomes hazardous and there was, moreover, desperate need for anything which could be converted into patrol craft. As fast as they came in from fishing voyages the big tunaboats were taken up for war service, painted gray and armed with depth-charges and machine-guns. Designated as "Yard craft—Patrol", each now carried on its bows a number preceded by the letters Y P, and immediately the term "Yippee Boats" came in.

Now the Navy had the boats, but it needed men to run them. The word was passed among the local fishermen, and at a mass meeting in the Naval Reserve Armory early in 1942, the personnel of the Navy was boosted by some 600 officers and men. They served in coastal waters and then, as the pressure decreased, boats and crews were sent out into the South Pacific. Their refrigerator equipment made them ideal for handling perishable stores, and the huge bait-tanks could haul fresh water to islands which had none. There were 47 of them pressed into service for carrying everything from fresh meat to ammunition—and to land raiding parties on enemy-held islands. Of the flotilla which went out from San Diego, 14 did not return; they had been lost by enemy action or by normal marine casualties.

At the end of the war, those which were left were turned back to their owners. Now radar and other sophisticated gear had become standard equipment and the fleet ranged even further beyond the horizon, even down to the West Coast of South America. Although traditionally hook-and-line operators, most of the San Diego fishermen were forced, by the exigencies of competition, to convert to the controversial purse-seine net.

They have come a long way, since the days of the junk and the salmon-boat and the little "one-lunger" which used to putt-putt out past Point Loma and bring in barracuda. So far as the fresh fish market-boats are concerned, hardly a dozen remain today; more fish, in fact, is brought in by truck from Mexico than is unloaded from the local fresh fish fleet. You can still buy pompano in San Diego if you know where to look for it, but it comes in from Florida by refrigerated air-express. And if you'll read the fine print at the bottom of that can of sardines put up by California packers, it may be a bit of a jolt to observe that it says "Product of South West Africa."

11. In the Wake of the *Cyane*

They're a lusty crowd and they're vastly proud
Of the slim, swift craft they drive,
Of the roaring flues and the humming screws
Which make her a thing alive.

—BERTON BRALEY

At midnight of July 28, 1846, the U. S. S. *Cyane*, Capt. Samuel F. Dupont U. S. N., commanding, hove-to in the blackness somewhere to the south-westerly of Point Loma, and nothing was further from the minds of her people than the thought that within a little over half a century "... the roaring flues and the humming screws ..." of an outlandish craft called a "torpedoboat-destroyer" would be putting San Diego on the map as a Navy town.

Land was picked up at 6:30 in the morning, and setting everything to the royals they headed for the harbor entrance, barely making steerageway. Then the morning breeze came up and by 8 a.m. she was logging a comfortable 5 knots; at 10:30 they shortened down to topsails and staysails, and the log reads: "... at 11:30 came too (sic) with the Starbd. anch. in 9½ fathoms water Point Gujarrs [Guijarros—now Ballast Point] bearing p. Compass S ½ W ..."

Thus came the United States Navy to San Diego, and the entries for the next 4-hour watch are of historic significance: "Commencing with moderate breezes from the W'ly and pleasant—at 3 the launch and alligator under command of Lieut. Rowan armed & Equipped and the Marine Guard under command of Lt. Maddox left the ship to take possession of the Town of San Diego & hoist the American Flag..."

To the landsman, a ship's log can be confusing. It was customary in those

---

*On the next page: Having lost most of her deck-load of coal a few hundred miles out of San Francisco, the U. S. S. Monterey, coast-defense monitor, put in to San Diego for more, in the summer of 1898. Here she is, off the Coal Bunkers Wharf, with sacked coal around the base of her turret. She has, of course, no radio antenna—but the four lanterns, hung vertically down her mast, show that at least she was rigged for night signalling by the old Ardois system of red-and-white lights.—*HISTORICAL COLLECTION, TITLE INSURANCE & TRUST CO.

days to start the "sea" day at noon rather than at midnight, and that "Commencing with moderate breezes . . ." entry starts the *sea* day of July 30—at noon of July 29, civil time. On one embarrassing occasion this led the good people of San Diego to observe the flag-raising anniversary on July 30, with ceremonies and speeches in the Old Town Plaza. The word "alligator" has done mischief, as well. Although the log clearly reads that ". . . at 3 the launch and alligator . . . left the ship . . ." and neither "launch" nor "alligator" is capitalized, historians have assumed that the latter was meant to be a proper name, despite the fact that a ship's boats are not named. So we get such accounts as ". . . the launch and *Alligator* . . ." An alligator, in addition to being a nasty creature with sharp teeth, also was a special type of landing-craft—just as today it is a special boat with a crane or derrick, used for handling logs.

So the *Cyane* contributed her bit of history by bringing the Navy to San Diego and San Diego to the United States, and went on about her business; she was decommissioned at Mare Island Navy Yard Sept. 20, 1871, and was sold at auction July 30, 1887. Soon after the *Cyane* came the famous old *Congress,* whose carpenter while here made a carriage for the Spanish cannon *El Jupiter,* cast in Manila in 1791 and which, while mounted at Fort Guijarros, no doubt was one of those which lobbed roundshot at the impudent *Lelia Byrd* in 1803. The gun then was hauled up to raw, new Fort Dupont on Presidio Hill, to defend San Diego; the fort, named for Captain Dupont of the *Cyane,* soon became Fort Stockton in honor of Commo. Robert F. Stockton U. S. N., whose flag the *Congress* flew and who outranked Dupont.

Other Navy vessels would call, at such widely spaced intervals that their arrivals would be of importance—as would also be the visits of the Revenue Cutter Service (now the Coast Guard) and of the Coast Survey, whose ships then were Navy-manned. And with their visits San Diego would witness the passing of a robust era, as hulls of oak were replaced by ones of iron and then of steel, while sails gave way as motive-power to such oddities as the horizontal compound engine of the U. S. S. *Hartford* and down through the triple-expansion and the turbine, and finally to atomic power.

What occupied the Navy originally was surveying. The West Coast of the United States and of Latin America had been charted badly if at all, and so, for the benefit of any and all mariners, the Navy set about to correct this. Few are the navigators who have not seen that line of tiny type at the bottom of a Mexican or Central American chart, with some such message as "*Based on Surveys by the U. S. S. Ranger, 1873*".

A whimsical beginning to local hydrography was the visit of the U. S. S. *Active* to San Diego in 1856. She had been surveying Cortes Bank, far to the westerly of Point Loma, when the Commanding Officer's wife—the Old Man's Missus was allowed aboard at sea, in those days—became nervous because of what she regarded as doubtfulness of their position, and ordered the captain to order the ship into some safe harbor. The hospitable natives gave a ball in honor of the occasion and the *Active's* officers replied in kind, as recounted by a tongue-in-cheek junior officer who kept a diary containing this notation: "Several took offense at not being invited and got up an opposition ball, which was a hard old affair and broke up in a fight."

Unexpectedly, the U. S. S. *Narragansett* put in at San Diego in the summer of 1873 because of an ailing air-pump, and of being a bit short on coal. Before she returned to her survey work she had made many friends, although far too little notice was taken of her somewhat retiring, 36-year-old commanding officer, who already had behind him active duty at Donaldsonville and at Fort Fisher, on the North Atlantic Blockade, and with Farragut in the Battle of New Orleans. A quarter of a century later his name would be on Page One all around the world and he would give a brief order destined to become a classic: "You may fire when ready, Gridley." He was Comdr. George Dewey U. S. N., the 1898 hero of Manila Bay.

That same summer San Diego was visited by the Revenue Cutter *Oliver Wolcott*; her C.O. was Capt. C. M. Scammon, after whom Scammon's Lagoon in Baja California is named, and whose contributions to the knowledge of whales and whaling are significant. But he had visited San Diego before; he first came in on November 5, 1872, in command of the Revenue Cutter *Wyanda*.

The U. S. S. *Tuscarora* got a conquering hero's welcome when she arrived on March 2, 1880—not because she was doing a good job of surveying along the Lower Coast, but because she had found and rescued nine shipwrecked San Diego fishermen who otherwise probably would have died of starvation. Just a month before, San Diego had received a maiden-voyage visit from the Navy-manned Coast Survey steamer *Carlile P. Patterson;* one of the earliest vessels specifically designed for oceanographic work, she returned to San Diego many years later as the U. S. S. *Forward*. That was in 1918, and she was on patrol duty along the Mexican coast.

Farragut's old flagship, the U. S. S. *Hartford*, made San Diego on Dec. 16, 1886, on her way to Mare Island for decommissioning; in later years, after rebuilding, she paid other calls. She drew big crowds and did the Navy no harm at all from a public-relations standpoint. Not only did her band put on a free concert, but the local police gratefully described her liberty-party as the most peaceful and orderly they had even seen. And they had a good yardstick by which to go; the *Ranger's* crew had been in port shortly before, and after a few nights of assorted hell-raising in Stingaree, The Law was not a bit sorry to see them depart.

And now came the white-hulled, steel ships of "The New Navy". On Oct. 6, 1892, the U. S. S. *Charleston* and *Baltimore*, of the first "White Squadron", arrived and while at San Diego put on a display which then was viewed with wonder but today doesn't even get a second look—night signalling by search-light. This was, of course, the old one-funnel *Charleston*, famous for her pursuit of the stolen steamer *Itata;* she was lost on Roncador Reef a few years later.

On Dec. 15, 1897, the monitor *Monterey* arrived on her way to Magdalena Bay, 600 miles south, for target-practice, and another monitor, the U. S. S. *Monadnock*, visited shortly afterward. The *Monterey* was back on June 21, 1898, but now she was painted battle-gray and was on her way to Manila to parade her impressive 12-inch guns before foreign vessels which had swarmed in after Dewey's victory and one of which in particular, the German, was becoming something of a problem.

For many years San Diego was considered as primarily a "destroyer port" and literally hundreds of that class have, at one time or another, called it home; the first two destroyers to enter the harbor were, however, British rather than American. Although we had a number of the smaller torpedo-boats, and some destroyers had been laid down, it was not until after the turn of the century that they were delivered. Meanwhile, on Boxing Day—Dec. 26—of 1897, H.M.S. *Virago*, one of Britain's first destroyers, steamed in past Point Loma while en route from England to the Naval Base at Esquimalt, B.C. She was a four-stacker of 300 tons displacement, armed with two 12-inch torpedo-tubes, a 12-pounder Armstrong and five Hotchkiss 6-pounder rapid-fire guns, and she was good for 30 knots. Her sister-ship, H.M.S. *Sparrowhawk*, came in on Jan. 3, 1898; they were escorted by two cruisers, H.M.S. *Leander* and *Phaeton*.

With only 26 feet of water over the bar and with Middleground Shoal still there in all its glory, the larger Navy ships avoided San Diego Bay and anchored off Coronado. When the "big" battleship *Iowa* anchored there on Jan. 9, 1900, an excursion-boat tried to get a crowd of visitors aboard, but found it too rough for safety. And when Rear Adm. Robley D. Evans' "Great White Fleet" arrived on April 14, 1908, there wasn't even a thought of bringing any of the sixteen battleships into the harbor. The fleet's destroyers, however, did come in, and San Diego has been rubbing elbows with des-troyers ever since. Those first ones were tiny by today's standards, being of only around 420 tons displacement and powered with "up-and-downers"— quadruple expansion reciprocating engines which gave them close to 30 knots. They were, of course, coal-burners.

There were larger vessels too, like the handsome little cruiser *Chicago*, flagship of the Pacific Squadron, and the second *Charleston* and her sister-ships, impressive with their four stacks. The first major vessel to come in was the U. S. S. *California*, an armored cruiser of 13,800 tons, on Dec. 4, 1910. Her Commanding Officer was Capt. Henry T. Mayo U. S. N., who four years later—the same year that the *California* was re-named *San Diego*— would make naval history at Vera Cruz. And in another four years she would hit a mine off Fire Island and go down, the Navy's only major casualty of the First World War.

The *California* having made it, other cruisers of her class came and went during the summer and fall of 1911—not always without "Middleground trouble"—as did an assortment of destroyers and support vessels, and the tiny submarines *Grampus* and *Pike*, first of their kind to visit San Diego. They were so small that they actually used to conduct exercises, submerged, right in San Diego Bay, and this was something of an annoyance to ferryboat captains—especially after one of them came up, almost under the old side-wheeler *Coronado*. It was a newsworthy event when one of them traveled, at periscope depth, from off the Santa Fe Wharf all the way out to the harbor entrance.

It was appropriate that the distinction of being the first battleship to enter San Diego Bay should go to the grand old "Bulldog of the Navy", the U. S. S. *Oregon*, which came in and anchored on Nov. 28, 1911. A score of years later, almost to the day, the first of the huge aircraft carriers would come and anchor almost where the *Oregon* had been; that was the 33,000-ton U. S. S. *Saratoga*, on Nov. 7, 1931.

But, back to 1911: "Torpedo Wharf", a few hundred yards east of the ferry-slip at Coronado, now was the scene of steady activity for the little "broken-deck" destroyers, while the submarines and their tender took over the ferry wharf itself. Naval activity built up slowly but steadily until the outbreak of the First World War, when practically everything went to the Atlantic. The *Oregon* dropped in from time to time, as did other casuals; the liner *Harvard*, now in the dazzle camouflage of war, called on her way to European waters, as did John D. Spreckels' steam yacht *Venetia*. She would return a few years later, proudly displaying two gold stars on her funnel; each represented an enemy submarine, liquidated off Gibraltar by her depth-charges. San Diego got its pre-view of the famous "four-pipers", later to mean so much to the city in 1917, as the destroyers *Caldwell* and *Fairfax*, their age then measured in days rather than years, paused briefly on their way from Mare Island to the War Zone. North Pacific Steam's liner *Beaver* came in, but now she was the U. S. S. *Beaver*, mother-ship to a brood of submarines. San Diego already had seen the old cruiser *New York*, famous in the Battle of Santiago; now she was the *Saratoga* and later would become the *Rochester* when the aircraft carrier *Saratoga* robbed her of her name, just as the then new battleship *New York* had done. Other war-time casuals would include the U. S. S. *Carl Schurz* (the captured German gunboat *Geier*) and a couple of big British merchantmen, hastily converted into cruisers.

After the war came the real influx. On Aug. 7, 1919 the new Pacific Fleet arrived, led by the U. S. S. *New Mexico*, flagship of Adm. Hugh Rodman U. S. N. With her were the battleships *Arizona* and *New York* which, like her, anchored outside—but two smaller battleships, the *Vermont* and the

Georgia, which had anchored off Coronado with Evans' fleet in 1908, calmly steamed in, as did the scout-cruiser *Birmingham,* support vessels, and more than 100 of the "four pipe" destroyers. The old East Santa Fe Wharf became San Diego's first big Destroyer Base and remained so for many months, until they moved to the re-vamped "concrete shipyard" at the foot of Thirty-second Street. One by one, most of them were "moth-balled"—and Red Lead Row came into being.

And again the war clouds lowered; fighting ships were needed, and Red Lead Row supplied them. Destroyers were hauled out one by one for the removal of barnacles; gray paint was slapped over the red preservative, long-cold boilers were checked and lighted off, and ships came to life again both for our own Navy and for the British, under Lend-Lease. The tempo built up and then, on the forenoon of Dec. 7, 1941, radio operators afloat and ashore logged that historic message—

AIR RAID ON PEARL THIS IS NO DRILL

Too late, people began to think of unheeded warnings. The Second World War had been dropped on our doorstep.

Now the curtain of censorship shut down on all ship movements and a word new to California—"convoy"—came into common use. On one occasion the Matson liners *Lurline, Monterey* and *Mariposa* all were in port together, but now they were troopships calling to lift personnel for Hawaii. All ships were running without lights; barrage-balloons appeared in the sky, military installations were fenced off with barbed-wire and anti-aircraft guns sprouted up everywhere. Countless tons of stores, tens of thousands of men moved through the port, for the Navy had not neglected its shore bases for supplies and communications and personnel, during the years which had passed.

The Navy's first shore installation had been what originally was called the Naval Wireless Station on Point Loma. That was in the spring of 1906, and even before it was formally commissioned the station had carried important traffic having to do with the disastrous earthquake and fire at San Francisco on April 18 of that year. The Coaling Station pier at Point Loma was built two years later and eventually got its gaunt, black, coal-loading tower—not too long before oil supplanted coal as the Navy's fuel. The temporary Naval Training Station of the First World War, in Balboa Park, had moved to vastly expanded quarters, also at Point Loma, and the Naval Air Station on North Island, the Naval Hospital in Balboa Park, and the Naval Supply Depot at the foot of Broadway had come into being, as had the Marine Corps Base (later the Marine Recruit Depot) and outlying training and communications facilities. The Eleventh Naval District, composed of the Southern California counties, the states of Arizona and New Mexico and the southerly tip of Nevada, was established Jan. 20, 1921; just a year before, the San Diego area had been made a Naval Operating Base under the Twelfth Naval District with headquarters in San Francisco.

The era of the Second World War would see strange sights, as the Navy took over the waterfront and the control of all shipping. Middleground Shoal now was but a dimming and unhappy memory and instead of 26 feet of water over the bar there now was 42; already the biggest battleships—the *California, New Mexico, Texas* and others—had entered and departed as a routine matter, as had the aircraft carrier *Saratoga* and her sister-ship, the *Lexington.* The big transatlantic liner *Manhattan* would call, only now she was a troopship, the U. S. S. *Wakefield.* And with tankers in desperately short supply, a presidential decree would set aside the statute forbidding the entry of foreign-flag ships into the coastwise trade; San Diego would have oil delivered by, for instance, the Canadian tanker *Albertolite* and huge Norwegian whaling factory-ship *Thorshammer.* Landing craft and other sophisticated types—command-ships, attack transports and the like—would appear in increasing numbers.

The war ended, to be succeeded by an uneasy peace, and the Old Navy was gone for all time. Destroyers now were as big as some of the early cruisers, and it is difficult to keep track of all of the exotic types which slip in and out of the harbor today, bristling with missile-launchers and every conceivable type of radar and other electronic gear. The little old *Cyane* of 1846? She was of a modest 792 tons, and a shade over 132 feet long. Perhaps it's just as well that old Captain Dupont had no crystal ball with which to look ahead for 121 years—to Sept. 16, 1967, when the U. S. S. *Enterprise,* aircraft carrier, came in and went much farther up the bay than he had done. Her full-load displacement is 85,850 tons and her over-all length is 1,102 feet.

Given the right gear, she could just about hoist the *Cyane* aboard.

12. Unsung Hero of the *Bennington*

...above and beyond the call of duty...
—CONGRESSIONAL MEDAL OF HONOR

It was stifflingly hot in the forward port fire-room of the United States gun-boat *Bennington* as she lay to an anchor in San Diego Bay on that July morning back in 1905.

A dim incandescent bulb and the orange glare from her fire-doors lit the compartment, where stokers heaved scoops of coal into the roaring furnaces, and the whole space hummed to the sound of bubbling water inside the massive boiler. The water-tender on watch, not long before, had sent a coal-passer up to shut off a small valve which vented air from the top of the boiler as the steam developed. In the semi-darkness he found two valves and, being inexperienced, closed both of them so that he could be sure he had shut off the right one. It was to prove a tragic, fatal mistake, for one of the valves led to the steam-gauge on the face of the boiler.

The fires roared on, the humming increased. At the rate things were going, soon the safety-valve might be lifting as the working-pressure of 250 pounds was reached and passed. The water-tender glanced at the thick glass tube of the water-gauge, which showed that the water in the boiler was at the right level. Then his eyes moved to the steam-gauge, and he was puzzled to note that the brass needle was still on zero. Oh, well—probably a bit of rust or sediment had got in and had, in some way, affected it.

The sweating stokers poured on the coal; they must have plenty of steam, for soon the *Bennington* would be winding in her anchor and getting under-way for Mare Island. The blank, expressionless "O" on the steam-gauge continued to puzzle, but not to alarm him; after all, there was a safety-valve on the boiler, wasn't there?

The muted rumble, the roar of the fires went on. Then there was another sound, an audible hissing and sputtering. He glanced up, to detect a lively feather of steam coming out from one of the seams—but the brass needle of the gauge still showed no pressure. Now—too late—he was beginning to worry.

"Hey!" he called to one of the coal-passers, "Run up topside and get the boiler-maker! There's something wrong here!"

The man scampered up the hot steel ladder and tumbled out onto the open deck. And then the world ended.

It wasn't a sharp report; rather, it was a sudden, numbing concussion which shook the gunboat from keel to trucks as the crown-sheet of one of the boiler's three "fire-holes" collapsed and released a ton of boiling water into the fire-room, carrying with it grate-bars, hot coals, ashes, the fire-doors themselves and anything which was in the way. The jet effect of the escaping water—which, with pressure reduced to that of the atmosphere, instantly turned to steam—ripped the boiler loose from its saddles and sent it plummeting into the bulkhead of the next boiler-room. Massive sea-connections for condenser, sanitary system and the bilge- and fire-pumps snapped off like so much macaroni, and she began to flood with the cold water of the bay.

In seconds the huge volume of steam had penetrated every enclosed part of the ship; sixty-five men were killed outright, blown overboard to drown, or were so badly scalded that they died within a few days. Next to the *Maine*, it was the worst peace-time disaster in the Navy's history. Stunned crewmen, many themselves in agony, helped the wounded as best they could; the *Bennington* began to list, and escaping vapor from the ruptured steam-lines of the other boilers moaned a macabre dirge for the dying ship.

Among those who heard or felt the concussion ashore was Joe Brennan, mate-deckhand of the little steam tug *Santa Fe*, who had sneaked away to the Snug Harbor Saloon for a beer while Capt. Bob Morris was uptown on business. Brennan raced back to the tug, cast off her lines and darted into the pilot-house, yanking the brass bell-pulls of gong and jingle for *Ahead, full*. There was work to do, even for a diminutive tug with only two men—the mate-deckhand and the engineer-fireman—aboard.

L. J. "Whitey" Gauthier, chief bosn's mate, had been knocked into a corner of the superstructure but was unhurt. As he attempted to round up his gang and see what could be done, he heard through the swirling steam the *Bong!* of an engineroom gong alongside, and a call of "Anyone there to take my lines?" It was Brennan, bringing up the *Santa Fe*. Gauthier leapt to the side of the careening gunboat and, with a few others, quickly got the tug's lines secured. By now it was obvious that the *Bennington* was sinking, and would have to be beached quickly if further disaster were to be averted, but there was one big obstacle: the anchor was down, and there was no steam on the windlass to bring it up. To free her so that the tug could move her in toward shore, there was only one thing to do—someone would have to crawl

---

On the next page: Beached in shallow water, the morning after the disaster, the Benning-ton *has drawn a crowd of curious onlookers. The* Santa Fe *tug has brought the diving-barge and a floating derrick alongside. Behind her looms the grim, black mass of the Coal Bunkers, and the square-rigger with cockbilled yards is herself not without historical interest—the British ship* Brabloch, *last of the once imposing fleet of windjammers to bring in coal from Australia. She had arrived a week before the explosion.*—HISTORICAL COLLEC-TION, TITLE INSURANCE & TRUST CO.

[63]

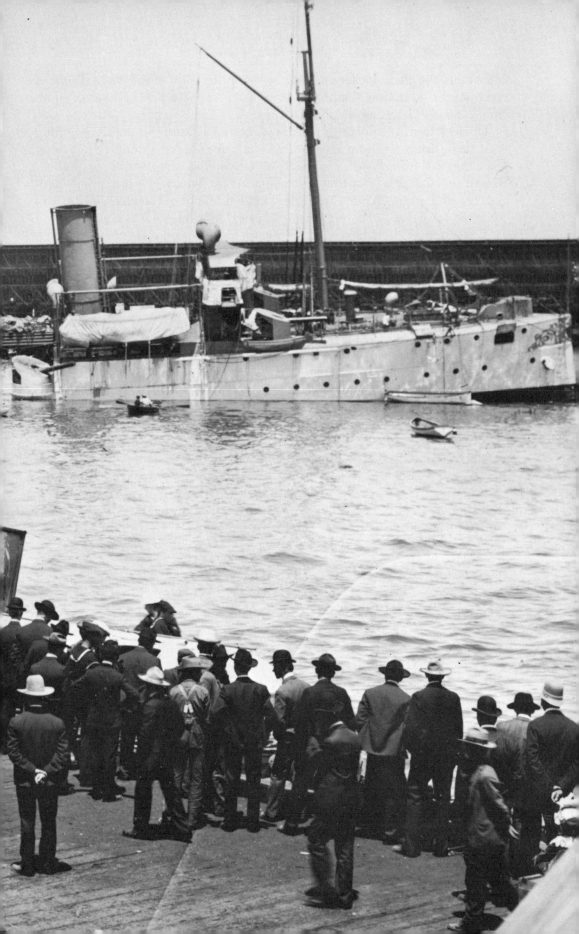

down into the chain-locker and release the "bitter end" of the chain. Without an instant's hesitation, Gauthier seized a fire-axe and plunged out of sight, into a cloud of live steam.

On deck they heard, faintly, the blows of his axe as he cut the stout lashing and then, like a writhing serpent, the chain roared out through the hawse-pipe. Again the *Santa Fe's* gong and jingle-bell rang, and the sinking gunboat began moving slowly in toward shallow water, where she grounded. Red-faced and gasping, Whitey Gauthier crawled up out of the chain locker and onto the open deck, exhaling steam. The next morning he was dead.

Launches, Whitehalls and skiffs swarmed toward the scene, their occupants dragging scalded but still swimming men—and those who would never swim again—from the bay. Two young men from the San Diego Rowing Club were in a wherry less than 100 yards away when she blew up, and they performed valiant service. The *Bennington's* own steam-launch, fortunately, had not yet been hoisted in and secured, and was kept busy transporting the dead and wounded to the float at the West Santa Fe Wharf. Horse-drawn hacks, buggies and even express-wagons were commandeered to get wounded and dying men to the soon overcrowded hospitals, for San Diego was a small city in 1905. A grisly tale was told of two undertakers, each anxious to be the first on the scene, racing their horses at a gallop down unpaved D Street (now Broadway), the town's main thoroughfare. Emergency hospitals were set up near the waterfront, and the response of doctors to the call for help was unanimous.

The coal-passer who had been sent up to find the boilermaker was the only one of her black-gang to survive. Subsequent investigation revealed that the stem of the old-fashioned lever-and-weight safety-valve, obviously not tested for months or perhaps even for years, was so "frozen" in place by rust and corrosion that it could not even be pried loose with a crow-bar.

Today, safety-valves are inspected and tested at regular and frequent intervals. The reform, however, came too late for the men who lie at the foot of a slender granite obelisk—the Bennington Monument—at the Fort Rosecrans National Cemetery on Point Loma, overlooking the scene of the disaster of July 21, 1905.

13. Of Steamships Large and Small

On account of this being steamer day, the formal opening of the Russ Public School building has been postponed until tomorrow. It is hoped there will be a large attendance.
—The San Diego Union, JULY 18, 1883

Steamer-wise, a lot of things have happened in San Diego during the century and more which has slipped away since that first tiny passenger liner, the *Oregon,* paddled in past Point Loma in the hectic year of 1849.

Wooden vessels, creaking in every joint to the action of the sea, and laying down a broad ribbon of froth from their paddle-wheels, were the thing for a long time; in fact the *Ancon,* last of the paddlers, hung on until the early 1890s. Staterooms were small and stuffy, and it was not unknown to find your bunk occupied not only by yourself, but by entomological specimens of one kind or another. And it was a good idea to get aboard soon enough to at least try to line up a seat for something better than the third sitting in the too small dining-saloon. But progress was on its way. The propeller replaced the paddle-wheels, the wooden hull was outmoded, and naval architects finally gave up designing staterooms which were exactly six feet—or maybe five feet ten—from bulkhead to bulkhead. Some of the more elegant bulkheads were made of what was called lincrusta—an embossed sheeting pressed from canvas impregnated in linseed oil—and it's a good thing that shipboard fires were not common. Stained glass in the skylights and clerestories of the Social Hall became increasingly flamboyant, and they even began to install that new-fangled invention, the electric light.

Scheduled coastwise service by steam began in 1851, when the sidewheeler *Goliah* came in from San Francisco for the first time. A former New York towboat built in 1849, she was hailed as the world's most powerful tug—but then came the Gold Rush; anything which could hold together until it got to California, and some which couldn't, headed for the lush trade in the Pacific. They built cabins onto the *Goliah,* sent her out via the Straits of Magellan, and for years she was San Diego's link with civilization, unless

you wanted to spend a week or more bouncing along the ludicrous wagon-trail to San Francisco in a stagecoach. Lt. George Horatio Derby, in *Phoenix-iana*, has left us some choice little items about his voyaging in the *Goliah;* when better passenger-steamers were available she was cut down to a tow-boat again and finally went to Puget Sound in 1871, where she lasted until 1899.

Moving in to share or pre-empt the profits of the *Goliah*, the *Constitution*, *Ohio*, *Quickstep* and *Sea Bird* began making San Diego calls from San Francisco via Monterey, Santa Barbara and San Pedro, and in 1854 the California Steam Navigation Co., famous for its Sacramento and San Joaquin River steamers, extended to San Diego. They kept it up until 1867 and brought, among others, the famous *Orizaba* and *Senator* to the San Diego run. Meanwhile—in 1854—Pacific Mail had received permission to drop San Diego and Monterey from its San Francisco-Panama schedule, so long as other adequate local service was available. Ben Holladay, of the California, Oregon & Mexico Steamship Co., bought out California Steam's coastwise service in 1867, and a year later merged the two into the North Pacific Transportation Co. He in turn sold out to Pacific Mail in 1872 and they maintained the coastal ships for three years, when they disposed of the local service to Goodall, Nelson & Perkins of San Francisco, which in 1876 incorporated as the Pacific Coast Steamship Co. By 1880 they were putting a steamer in to San Diego every five days, using the *Orizaba*, *Ancon* and *Senator* in the passenger and express freight service, augmented by such smaller freighters as the *Constantine*, *Bonita* and *Santa Cruz*—nicknamed "hog boats" because they frequently transported hogs and other livestock.

But the wooden side-wheelers were on their way out, and screw steamers with long, skinny iron hulls took over. The famous *Queen of the Pacific* came out in 1882—her name was shortened to *Queen* in 1890—and the two-stacker *Santa Rosa*, with auxiliary barkentine rig, appeared in 1884. Much was made of the fact that they had electric lights—just as the *Queen* later got onto Page One, in mid-November of 1907, by being the first wireless-equipped merchant vessel to enter port. When the *City of Puebla* (not *Pueblo*) arrived on her maiden voyage, Feb. 3, 1888, there was mention of a novelty in her dining-saloon; in addition to the traditional long tables, there were several "private" tables, seating only seven each. In command on this voyage was Capt. Ezekiel Alexander, formerly of the *Ancon* and later, for many years, the popular master of the *Santa Rosa*. The famous old *Orizaba*, of the oaken frames and chestnut planking, was gone; gone, too was her best-known master, Capt. Henry James (Ninety Fathom) Johnston, who bought sage-

In 1912, travel was slower but more fun. Relaxing on the forward deck of the President *are San Diego-bound passengers—including, between the ventillators, the well-dressed tourist, complete with golf cap and Gates Ajar collar, who seems to be making big time with the ladies. Ah, these ship-board romances!—*SOCIETY OF CALIFORNIA PIONEERS

brush acreage overlooking San Diego Bay and was planning his retirement home there at the time of his unexpected death in 1878. His daughter started the house, Orizaba Villa, in 1887—the year the old side-wheeler was broken up—and the company gave her the steamer's dining-saloon sideboard and the railings of the companionway which led from the saloon up to the social-hall. Although extensively altered, the house still stands; the street on which it faces is Orizaba Ave., and its owner points with pride to that handsome railing, leading up from the entrance-hall. A former owner of the house cherishes that sideboard, and up until not too many years ago one of the steamer's deck-houses served as quarters for the lighthouse-keeper at New York Slough, up-river from San Francisco.

The red Maltese cross in a white diamond on a blue field, the house-flag of the Pacific Coast Steamship Co., was a familiar sight for sixty years, although four white stars were added in 1916 when the line merged with H. F. Alexander's Admiral Line and became the Pacific Steamship Co. New and larger ships of steel meanwhile had augmented or replaced the old iron ones. The 5,433-ton *Governor* and *President* came out in 1907, replacing the *Santa Rosa* and her popular running-mates *Queen* and *State of California* on the regular San Diego service. They built the larger *Congress* in 1913; a ship of many fates, she burned out in 1916 and was sold, becoming China Mail's *Nanking*. Later she returned to Pacific Steam as the *Emma Alexander* and was, with the stately *Ruth Alexander*, the last of a glorious era when, in 1936, coastal passenger service was killed for all time by rail and bus competition, and a proliferation of capricious maritime strikes. The *Santa Rosa* stranded near Point Arguello in 1911; the *State of California* hit a pinnacle rock in Alaska in 1913 and took 31 of her 139 people down with her; the *Governor* sank in Puget Sound in 1921 with the loss of nine lives, after colliding with the *West Hartland*. Early in the Second World War a Japanese bomber got the *Ruth Alexander* down around the Philippines, and the *Emma Alexander*, now British and with the dreadful name of *Empire Woodlark*, was one of the futile convoy which was too late to save Singapore. In 1947 the Ministry of Transport loaded her up with the gas-bombs which the Allies had stockpiled but had not been obliged to use, and scuttled her in mid-Atlantic.

There were many others as well. In 1910 the swift, triple-screw turbiners *Yale* and *Harvard* came out via the Straits of Magellan and put on a real express passenger and package-freight service between San Diego, Wilmington and San Diego; you left San Diego at 9 a.m. today and at 10 tomorrow morning you were in San Francisco. The service, originally under the Pacific Navigation Co., was disrupted by the First World War, but the two ships came back unharmed, ran for a while under the Admiral Line house-flag and then were taken over by the Los Angeles Steamship Co., who maintained four sailings a week until the *Harvard* was wrecked at Point Arguello in 1931. They brought the *Iroquois* out from the east coast to take her place, but she wasn't fast enough and they sent her home six months later; bravely the *Yale* kept on, alone, until the 1936 strike.

In 1915 the North Pacific Steamship Co. appeared as rivals on the San Diego run, using the *Roanoke* and the *George W. Elder*—which in the 1880s had served San Diego under the colors of Pacific Coast Steam. And in 1911 the McCormick Steamship Co., a branch of the Charles R. McCormick Lumber Co., started running its steam-schooners, with passenger accommodations, into San Diego from Pacific Northwest ports via San Francisco and San Pedro. They were small, wooden steamers, with three berths in most of the staterooms, but the food was good and the all-inclusive fare was so low that it was cheaper to travel than to stay at home.

At the peak of its glory, the Admiral Line had both a Columbia River and a Puget Sound service to San Diego. On Sunday morning it was the *Emma Alexander* or the *Ruth Alexander* for Wilmington, San Francisco, Seattle and Victoria, B.C., and Monday night would see the *Admiral Benson* or the *Admiral Peoples* leaving for Wilmington, San Francisco, and Portland, Ore.; with the *Yale* out for San Francisco every Tuesday and Friday and the *Harvard* every Sunday and Thursday, it gave San Diego six passenger sailings to the north every week.

Neither of James J. Hill's big liners *Great Northern* or *Northern Pacific* were regular San Diego callers, although both called on their way out from the East Coast to go on the Los Angeles-San Francisco-Astoria run, and the *Great Northern*, re-named *H. F. Alexander*, paid occasional visits in later years; her one-day stop on her maiden voyage was on Feb. 10, 1915. The *Northern Pacific*, which had not intended to call, came in under rather unhappy circumstances on April 8; a passenger had smallpox. Ordinarily, if there is a case of smallpox in a liner, the patient is the youngest of eleven children of some unemployed caviar-maker coming to The Land of Freedom for a fresh start—but this time it was one of the more *de luxe* passengers, and how he got it is anyone's guess.

For every passenger steamer there were many cargo-carriers. Tiny steam schooners like the *Newsboy* and the *West Coast* brought lumber from the dog-holes of Mendocino and as the lumber industry grew so did they, into Hanify's and Hart-Wood's big wooden three-gear steamers, and Hammond's and Phillips' steel four-masters, worked over from Shipping Board "Lake" type freighters. In the oil trade the scow-schooners *Caesar Bruns* and *San Pedro*, carrying oil in barrels, would give way to Union Oil's pine-hulled schooner *Santa Paula* and barkentine *Fullerton* (with wooden oil tanks, no less!) and to Standard Oil's barges. Then would come the steel tankers— *Whittier, Argyll, Capt. A. F. Lucas, Oleum* and *S. C. T. Dodd*, to name a few. Later would come the big T-2 tankers of Second World War vintage, under the colors of Union and Richfield and Standard, and Star & Crescent's unromantic but efficient steel barges, towed by Diesel tugs. Not the least interesting of them was the slim, engines-amidships tanker *Argyll*, later the

Panamanian *San Luciano;* when she was wrecked in 1965 she was 73 years old.

American-Hawaiian Steamship Co. pioneered the intercoastal freight service in 1907 with its big "Tehuantepec Route" steamers, and for the next seven or eight years such names as *Isthmian, Alaskan, Mexican* and *Kansan* were familiar in San Diego. Cargo from the East Coast was shipped in corresponding steamers down to Coatzacoalcos at the southern end of the Gulf of Campeche, carried by rail across the Isthmus of Tehuantepec and re-loaded in the line's Pacific freighters at Salina Cruz, for delivery in San Diego (then still the main port for Southern California) and San Francisco. Completion of the Panama Canal—and, more significantly, of Los Angeles Harbor—ended that service.

But if the Panama Canal took one service away from San Diego it was, a few years later, to give her others, the best known of which was the Panama Pacific Line, bringing passengers and fast freight from New York via Havana and Panama. First of their ships to call was the former transatlantic liner *Finland*, of around 12,000 tons, on Aug. 20, 1915. She brought the first passengers to land in San Diego by a regularly scheduled service from the East Coast, and was running opposite her sister-ship, the *Kroonland*—but the First World War was approaching, and the service was of short duration.

It was not until 1924 that Panama Pacific returned to San Diego, with the *Finland* and *Kroonland* now running on a three-ship schedule with the former Pacific Mail transpacific liner *Manchuria*, of 15,400 tons; a few months later her sister-ship, the *Mongolia*, replaced the *Kroonland*. The three veterans served until the new turbine-electric liner *California* came out in 1927, followed by the *Virginia* and *Pennsylvania* the following year. The three were more-or-less sister-ships of around 18,000 tons and one of them made San Diego every second Friday, right up until the disastrous maritime strikes of 1934 and 1936 killed both the coastwise and intercoastal trade. They were sold to Moore-McCormack and ended their days in the South American trade, as the *Argentina, Brazil* and *Uruguay*. One of them was in San Pedro during the war, as a trooper; MorMac had removed her second funnel (which was a dummy) and it greatly improved her appearance.

Freighters were frequent, too, via the Big Ditch; Isthmain's gray-hulled steamers like the *Steel Ranger* and the *Birmingham City* called from Portland, Me., and way ports at frequent intervals. There was a Swayne & Hoyt ship at least once a month, out of the Gulf, and American-Hawaiian came back in the 1930s, from the southern Atlantic seaboard. Williams, Dimond & Co.'s Quaker Line lasted until long after the Second World War, and there were the Williams Line and—briefly—the Transmarine Line with its turbine freighters bearing horrendous names like *Sujerseyco* and *Sunewarkco* and *Sulanierco.*

Steamer Day may not hold the significance which it did when San Diego got its news of the outside world from a bundle of stale San Francisco newspapers brought ashore by a paddle-steamer's purser—but even today, a ship of unusual size or importance is a crowd-getter. The area around the Broadway and B Street Piers was sardine-packed when the 26,500-ton *Belgenland* made a one day cruise-stop on Dec. 31, 1930. When the nuclear-powered *Savannah* came in on Jan. 14, 1963, it led to several days in which San Diegans more-or-less patiently stood in line for hours, to get aboard. Six months later, on July 15, the P. & O. - Orient liner *Oriana*, of 42,000 tons, quietly slid in alongside Broadway Pier and if you were a pedestrian in that area you didn't go where you wanted to go—you went where the crowd went.

Never again, however, will you go from San Diego to San Francisco for $10, berth and meals included—or $9, for that matter, if you took a steam schooner. The white-hulled *Yale* making fast at Broadway Pier at exactly 8 p.m., with her orchestra whanging out "Rose Marie", is a sweet but fading memory. Grizzled gourmets still recall nostalgically the prime rib you got in the *Emma Alexander*, that superb apple pie aboard the *Admiral Peoples*, those tender little steaks served up in the dining-saloon of the *Yale* or the *Harvard*—and did you ever try the galantine of turkey listed on the menu of a Panpac liner? It was not food, it was poetry.

Now, as the Pacific Coast rolls away thousands of feet below, you balance a trayful of plastic dinnerware on your knees. There is no Captain's Table nor Chief Engineer's Table, not even your own table. But there's a curvaceous blonde hostess flitting up and down the aisle, making sure that your paper cup is kept full of coffee.

Well, Mac—that's progress. And you can have it.

14. Hanky-Panky

A bare foot pattered on deck
Ropes creaked; then—all grew still

—ALFRED NOYES

Back in the days when the water lapped against Atlantic St.—now Pacific Highway—the area at its southerly end and around the corner, down past the mud-flats of Little Venice, was not without its quota of men who regarded the laws on smuggling somewhat lightly. And it wasn't the safest place in town to go for an evening stroll.

As you might expect, it was the wily Yankee who introduced smuggling into California waters; in a sense, however, you could hardly blame him. Bumptious Spanish and Mexican officials had both their own laws and their own interpretation of those laws, and it would be naive to assume that the slyly outstretched hand, palm upward, was unknown. From the day of the sea-otter trade, down through that of smuggled cigars and Chinamen and on to the horrors of Prohibition, San Diego has not lacked for fast boats—not always showing their running-lights—and silent, poker-faced men who were adept at smuggling both out of, and into, Mexican waters.

So let us turn back to the summer of 1828, when we find the French trader *Le Heros*, Capt. Auguste Duhaut-Cilly, anchored off La Playa. Another trader, the American ship *Franklin*, is standing in from sea, and all unbeknown to her people, a rude reception is awaiting her.

When the Mexican customs people clambered aboard, Capt. John Bradshaw was informed that, thanks to couriers afoot and on mule-back, his activities along the Lower Coast were well known. He was told to unload his cargo into a warehouse, where he would be permitted to explain the legality of each and every item he had; his trading activities, it was alleged,

---

An immortal of the Seven Seas; the U. S. Revenue Cutter Bear *is airing her sails and her signal-flags in San Diego Bay in 1911; she visited on many occasions. Later she became a floating museum at Oakland; Rear Adm. Richard E. Byrd used her on an Antarctic expedition, and she wound up in Canada. There was some pretty sharp criticism when they lost her a few years ago, while attempting to tow her tired old hull from Halifax to Florida in winter, but there are those who feel that foundering in the Atlantic was a more fitting end to a glorious career than to have her wind up as a night club.*—HISTORICAL COLLECTION, TITLE INSURANCE & TRUST CO.

had been carried on without bothering about export duties or other fiscal trivia. Bradshaw agreed—but as soon as his visitors were safely ashore, he made sail for an anchorage just inside the harbor entrance; obviously, a quick get-away was in his mind.

At this point Gov. José Maria Echeandía ordered a squad of soldiers to board her, and was greatly chagrined when he found out that he had no boat big enough to carry them. While he was arranging to borrow a boat from the Frenchman, Bradshaw got wind of it and they wound in the anchor, made sail and started off. Fort Guijarros opened fire with what guns were in an operating condition and had cannon-balls which would fit; the ship took a bit of damage and Bradshaw was wounded, but they got away.

The end of Mexican rule in 1846 was followed by the setting up of an American Custom House at La Playa, appointment of a Collector of Port' and finally by assistance from vessels of the Revenue Cutter Service in establishing at least a token enforcement of smuggling laws. The cutter *Wyanda* would appear, and the *Richard C. Rush* and the *Thomas Corwin* and the *Thetis*. Later still would come the *Manning*, which based on San Diego in 1905-6, and the immortal *Bear*, whose home port was San Diego from 1909 to 1919, and again in 1922-23.

Christmas of 1879 was just around the corner when W. W. Bowers, the collector, picked up a rumble from his "intelligence network" that in some way smugglers had succeeded in getting 54,000 cigars ashore and into an abandoned barn in Chollas Valley. He swooped down on the barn and got the cigars, to the joy of the local population. What would become of the cigars? Why, they would be auctioned off by the U. S. Marshal; this Christmas, in San Diego, cigars would be both plentiful and cheap. However, they failed to reckon with bureaucratic procedure: the Custom House in San Francisco out-ranked the one at San Diego, and to San Francisco the cigars must go. With sincere sadness everyone, Bowers included, watched as they were loaded aboard the *Orizaba*, to be seen no more.

It says in the *List of Merchant Vessels of the U. S.* that the schooner *Lou* was built in San Diego in 1883, but this is not so; she was *re*-built in San Diego from an archaic, double-ended sloop called *Newhope*, reputedly brought around Cape Horn in 1849 on the deck of a ship. The *Lou* is important, for if there was any kind of skulduggery in which she was not from time to time engaged, it was because certain of her owners just hadn't thought of it. They were always after her for something, but seldom with success—and this was just as true in Mexican as in American waters. She would brazenly bring in contraband Chinese at Point A while lawmen, armed to the teeth, lay in wait for her at Point B, and then go down into Mexico to poach guano or to smuggle in lard, matches or anything else which carried a high import duty.

The Mexicans hated her. On one occasion the *comandante* at Ensenada chartered the little steamer *Manuel Dublan,* loaded her to the guards with soldiers, and sent her out to seize the *Lou,* reportedly somewhere down around Cedros Island. He was fuming over a recent incident in which the *Lou* had been captured and brought into Ensenada. They had left the two-man crew aboard, warning them that their anchor-light would be under continuous watch from ashore, and if they had any idea of sneaking away—ah, *señores,* how unfortunate it would be if we were obliged to use the artillery! So the night wore on and then, as they used to put it in the days of the silent movies, Came The Dawn—but minus the *Lou.* Her anchor-light was still burning, but it hung from an upended boat-hook in the schooner's skiff. She had slipped and run.

The *Manuel Dublan* found the *Lou* and with due formality the skipper was placed under arrest, despite his protests that he was on an innocent trading-voyage. And the schooner, with an armed guard detail aboard, was taken in tow for the triumphal return to Ensenada. At dusk the uninvited guests were served a foul meal; meanwhile the wind was rising, it was cold, and the *Lou* rolled abominably. The soldiers frantically signalled to the steamer and were taken aboard; then the towing was resumed, in the now inky darkness. A gray and cheerless dawn revealed to the unhappy people in the steamer that they now were all alone, and when they hauled in the tow-line it was seen to be neatly severed. In that wind, the tiny schooner could be any number of miles away, in any one of at least 180 directions. Sadly they went on to Ensenada, were appropriately chewed out by the *coman-dante* and resumed their interrupted voyage to San Diego. There the American Customs men found, in an officer's stateroom, some hundreds of cigars which he had neglected to declare, and which cost the ship a tidy fine.

The story of the *Itata* affair has been told too often to warrant detailed repetition here. Briefly, she was a Chilean steamer, operating for a revolutionary party, and she was supposed to rendezvous off the coast with a schooner bearing the unique name of *Robert and Minnie,* from which she would receive a cargo of arms for the *insurrectos.* But she came in to San Diego, having run low on coal, on May 3, 1891. The procurer of munitions, meanwhile, had become a bit gabby about his big deal, and suddenly the U. S. Marshal from Los Angeles appeared, accompanied by a San Francisco Private Eye who represented the then President of Chile. He seized her and put an armed deputy aboard.

Three days later there was a bit of Gilbert & Sullivan gunplay on the steamer's bridge, and she steamed out of port. The pilot (who was in on the deal) and the Marshall's man were put off in a small boat, and the next step came when the marshal, in some way, contrived to get the Navy involved. The cruiser *Charleston* set off in hot pursuit, caught up with her at Iquique and brought her back to San Diego, arriving on July 4. With the normal legal delays, the case against the *Itata* did not come up until the following March. Meanwhile the revolutionary party had triumphed in Chile, and poor old Uncle Sam was in the regrettable position of having backed the wrong horse. The government's case was thrown out, the *Itata* was released, and Chilean-American relations reached an all-time low. The *Itata*, in the manner of many old steamers, plugged along for years; then, on Aug. 29, 1922, she went down in a storm off Coquimbo, and of the 328 people aboard only six survived.

Then, there was the British tramp steamer *Maori King*, which came into port in 1907 with lots of trouble. Aboard her were 980 Chinese and 350 Russians and other nationalities, and they were really seething. It seems they had been loaded up at Vladivostok and were told that they were going to work on a railroad at Hongkong. After several days of steaming steadily eastward they got suspicious, and found out that they were in fact being transported to Guaymas, to work on Southern Pacific's lines in Mexico. Naturally they were upset about this, and a couple of hundred miles off the California coast they informed the captain that if land were not sighted by the next day, they were going to murder all of the officers and take over. So he put in at San Diego and took his troubles to, of all people, the Mayor. Would His Honor get him an Armed Guard? His Honor would.

The man selected to recruit the guard was Don M. Stewart, then a lieutenant in command of the local division of the Naval Militia of California. Of course, they couldn't act officially, but Stewart rounded up a score of adventurous characters, both militiamen and others, who agreed the ride the *Maori King* to Guaymas for $5 a day and found—and to provide their own shotguns. By frequent and conspicuous drill with their weapons, Stewart and his stalwarts averted a general rising of the Chinese, and the steamer made it to Guaymas and safety.

When the three-masted schooner *Annie Larsen* arrived from San Francisco on Feb. 3, 1915, it was an open secret that she was to load some 4,000 Krag-Jorgensen rifles, and ammunition variously reported as 40,000 rounds and 4,000,000 rounds, for delivery to some mysterious individual in Topolobampo, Mex. Actually, so the story goes, she was to rendezvous at sea with a steamer which would take the munitions to Bombay, for a German-planned revolution which, by giving the British another major headache, would relieve the pressure on the Kaiser's armies along the Western Front of the First World War. For the Germans, it would have been a good idea—if it had worked.

There was a cursory investigation which delayed things for three days, but the Topolobampo story apparently was accepted, and a temporary embargo on her cargo was lifted. She took her leisurely time and finally was towed to sea, ostensibly bound for Topolobampo—but a month later she showed up in Braithwaite Bay on Socorro Island, about 250 miles south-southwesterly from the tip of Baja California. Meanwhile British intelligence was doing its usual, workmanlike job—and into Braithwaite Bay popped H.M.S. *Newcastle*. As the schooner was flying the American flag and in Mexican waters, the cruiser's C.O. hesitated to seize her—but his advice to her master was brief and to the point: "You get to hell out of here!" And he got. From there on the plot went from bad to worse; they never made the rendezvous, they got into difficulties in a Mexican port and finally, months later, the wandering *Annie Larsen* showed up at Aberdeen, Wash. Her cargo was seized and sold at public auction, the master got into hot water because of the now somewhat ramshackle status of the schooner's papers, and at long last a trial resulted in several people, including a couple of San Diegans, doing a stretch in jail for neutrality violation.

Not always equipped with the best of ships, the Revenue Cutter Service plugged along its quiet way, being occupied mostly with the suppression of smuggling Chinese and narcotics. On Jan. 28, 1915, the Revenue Cutter Service and the Life Saving Service were merged to form today's Coast Guard, whose trim, white-hulled cutters continued to make San Diego a frequent port of call. Then came the First World War and, immediately afterward, the "noble experiment" of Prohibition.

It was too fast a game now for schooners—except for a big five-masted Canadian schooner, the *Malahat*, which served as the mother-ship for Rum Row and anchored in the lee of Cape Colnett, some 140 miles down the Mexican coast from San Diego, which was all perfectly legal. To her came the supply of liquor from Europe, in such craft as the British tramp steamers *Arwyco* and *Ray Roberts* and the German motorships *Nedried* and *Lillehorn;* up from Tahiti came the little French auxiliary schooner *Quand Meme* with cognac and absinthe. From the *Malahat* it was loaded into the moderate-speed "intermediate" boats like the ex-Navy submarine-chaser *Hurry Home,* which took it to within 20 miles or so of the California coast to transfer it, on dark nights, to the actual rum-runners—the *Agilis,* the *Yukatrivol* and the *Chief Skugaid,* for instance. A typical "runner" looked like a water-taxi, but was triple-screw. There was a Diesel on the center-line shaft, with which she could cruise indefinitely at eight or ten knots, but each outboard propeller was driven by a 900-horsepower Liberty motor, obligingly supplied from war surplus by the United States government for as little as $5 each. Their gasoline consumption was outlandish—but who worries about expense when he's got the Coast Guard on his tail?

And how the Coast Guard loved to catch one! The service was expected to do its job with relatively slow craft, but now and then they were in just the right spot to capture a "rummy"—and when they did she was confiscated, to don gray paint, machine-guns, a one-pounder and a Coast Guard number. And by tradition, the skipper of the patrolboat which had caught her became her new C.O.

The law was unpopular, and there was an over-supply of buyers for that real, genuine Scotch whisky. Some of its drinkers, however, would have been less than happy had they talked to any of the people from, for instance, the San Diego-based cutter *Tamaroa,* which used to annoy Rum Row by noseying around in a sort of War of Nerves. Morning after morning, they

[79]

said, you could see a string of empty Belgian 2-litre alcohol tins, drifting away from the *Malahat*. . . . Ah, that lovely Scotch whisky—fresh from the Highlands!

The service was not unhappy when Prohibition was repealed—even though they had been one of the few governmental agencies to weather that harrowing period without scandal. Happily, they still had their primary job of protecting life and property at sea, in a period which would see the number, but not always the skill, of yachtsmen increase explosively.

Aircraft now were an integral part of the organization, and the Coast Guard Air Station at San Diego was established May 4, 1934, in an unused hangar at Lindbergh Field. Now an injured or critically ill mariner who would otherwise probably have succumbed, could be air-lifted from hundreds of miles away, to a San Diego hospital. A few years later they got their own station with hangars, shops, living-quarters and office space, right on the water's edge, and added the handy helicopter to their kit of tools. On July 1, 1939 the Coast Guard took over the U. S. Lighthouse Service, oldest federal agency, and then the Steamboat Inspection Service.

The *Bear* and the *Manning* are gone, but their places were filled by the trim, turbo-electric *Itasca*, the Diesel-driven *Calypso* and *Perseus*, and a continuing string of others. If the ghost of the *Oliver Wolcott* were to steam into port today old Captain Scammon, her whale-wise C.O., would be proud of the Revenue Cutter Service's robust descendant.

15. "... and has not since reported."

The man who trudged into sleepy little San Diego on that pleasant July day in 1851 was weary, footsore and hungry—and badly in need of a bath. This was perfectly reasonable, for he had walked some 150 miles up the Mexican coast and he was bringing to San Diego its first story of a shipwreck in the American era.

Someone directed him to the office of the *San Diego Herald* where, after introducing himself, he handed a letter to Editor Ames. The letter was from a friend, Capt. James Marks of the little screw-steamer *Union*, presently ashore and destined to stay there, down around San Quintín. She had left San Francisco for Panamá on July 2, which gave her people two days to get organized for a proper observance of the Fourth of July. And organized they were, as of the night of July 4, so much so that the question has been raised as to whether her quartermaster knew that he was steering a steamer or a Concord stagecoach, and at 3 a.m. July 5 the poor little *Union* piled headlong onto the beach.

The weather was calm, and without incident her 250 passengers got ashore, together with their baggage and some of the gold in her cargo. One man volunteered to walk to San Diego for help, and luckily Pacific Mail's steamer *Northerner* came along about then, making San Diego southbound, and went to their aid. Passengers, baggage, gold and all were picked up July 24 for return to San Diego, and the story closed with a cheerful item in the *Herald:* "Mr. Sam L. Vought [the purser] of the steamer *Northerner* will please accept our thanks for files of the San Francisco papers and also the 'fixins' for the proper compounding of sundry whiskey punches."

San Diego's second shipwreck was closer to home and potentially far more serious. Northbound for San Francisco, the side-wheeler *Golden Gate*, with 750 people aboard, snapped her main shaft while off Baja California. This was on Jan. 10, 1854; she drifted for four days while her engineers performed

the not-too-easy task of getting her patched up so that they could get one of her paddle-wheels turning, and on Jan. 18 she was approaching the harbor entrance of San Diego. It was stormy, the wind was on her beam, and with only one wheel operating the problem of steering her quickly went from difficult to impossible; she grounded on Zuñiga Shoal, at the east side of the channel entrance.

The *Goliah* was in port and went to her aid, but couldn't move her. Now the wind increased; seas broke over the *Golden Gate*, the dining-saloon was flooded, a man fell down a hatch and was killed, and it's a miracle that she didn't break up. After many horrifying hours the wind eased and the steamer *Southerner* got a line on her and succeeded where the smaller *Goliah* had failed. Her passengers were transferred, and she was towed to San Francisco for repairs.

On the night of Dec. 9, 1872 the *Montana*, southbound, lay at Culverwell's Wharf. C. P. Taggart, the Pacific Mail agent, had just blown out the lamp over his desk and headed ashore for a belated supper when a ship's lifeboat came alongside and a stiff and weary man climbed out and went looking for him. He was T. Herrington, Second Officer of the side-wheeler *Sacramento*, and he had a message for Taggart from his skipper, Capt. E. L. Farnsworth. Not finding Taggart, Herrington took his message aboard the *Montana*—and that was the first they knew that shortly before midnight of Dec. 5 the northbound *Sacramento* had crashed onto an uncharted reef near San Geronimo Island, some 200 miles south. Herrington's boat, manned by two quartermasters and five Chinese sailors, had rowed the distance in four days.

The *Montana* was sent off to rescue her people, camped on the beach, and plans for salvage were made. Although she broke up only a few hours before the wrecking-master arrived with his gear, the gaunt timbers of her gallows-frame remained standing until well into the 1930s, over what the charts list as Sacramento Reef. Around 1962 some brass valves, which had been in her engineroom, were brought up by skin-divers.

Almost an even eight years later, and again of a cheerless winter evening, another lifeboat pulled up to Culverwell's Wharf—only by now it was Jorres' Wharf, and what had been Pacific Mail's office was occupied by A. Wentscher, shipping agent and German Consul. This latter was fortunate, for the name on the boat was *Johanna Heinrich* and the hailing-port was Hamburg. In the boat, and in a bad way from exposure and fatigue, were Capt. P. A. F. Clasen, Second Officer Wage and five sailors. The *Johanna Heinrich*, Hamburg for San Francisco, had foundered on the night of Nov. 17, 1880, about 300 miles west of San Luis Obispo; that was 16 days before,

---

To many San Diegans, it was like the death of an old friend when the iron steamship Santa Rosa *stranded at Point Arguello July 7, 1911, and broke up. For many years afterward, one of her boilers was still visible in the surf.*—HISTORICAL COLLECTION, TITLE INSURANCE & TRUST CO.

and about 550 miles from San Diego. The German ship had begun leaking during a storm, shortly after they rounded Cape Horn, and they had pumped continuously. Off the California coast another storm, and a worse one, hit them, and she really opened up. They abandoned ship, saw her go under, and headed for the coast in two boats, the second one containing First Officer Elfels, the carpenter, the cook and two boys. On the second night they lost contact, and Elfels' boat was never seen again.

The next two battered ships to put in at San Diego were German also. On Feb. 10, 1901, the San Francisco tug *L. Luckenbach* (which had called southbound to top off her bunkers) brought in the steel four-masted bark *Edmund* from Santa Rosalia, in the Gulf of California—leaking, top-hamper sent down, and with her donkey-boiler spouting steam from every tube, which was no help to the salvage-pumps which were keeping her afloat. She had gone on the beach at the Mexican copper port and had punctured a plate; eight times they had pumped her out and eight times they had to let her fill and settle again, to keep her from pounding to pieces as one "norther" after another came up. On the ninth try they made it, but not by much.

The German ship *Otto Gildemeister*, of many names, was not far behind. Dismasted and hundreds of miles south of her course, she was found off Oceanside by the steam schooner *National City* and was towed in on Feb. 23, 1901; she had been on a passage from Yokohama for Portland, Ore. A few days later the Spreckels tug *Defiance*—which, as the *L. Luckenbach*, had just brought in the *Edmund*—came down to get her. The *Otto Gildemeister* originally was the British ship *Zemindar;* after repairs she beame the American bark *Homeward Bound* and revisited San Diego, with a load of lumber, in 1907. Later she was, for many years, the Alaska Packers' *Star of Holland*, before winding up as a Canadian sawdust barge.

The eerie glimmer of a pyrotechnic flare, through the slashing rain on the night of Dec. 31, 1909, was the first indication to Keeper William Beeman, of Point Loma Lighthouse, that the three-masted schooner *Alice McDonald* was in trouble, and almost in his own front yard. By the shaky telephone line to Fort Rosecrans he got the word in to town and the tug *Bahada*, the Revenue Cutter *Bear* and the visiting tug *Dauntless*, in with an oil-barge, went to her aid, but there was nothing they could do in that gale. The next day a line was floated down to her from windward, using an empty oil-drum as a buoy; when the wind went down much of her full load of lumber was lightered off, and eventually she was freed. Seven years later, the writer clambered aboard her hulk on Oakland Creek's Rotten Row, and wished that they had left her to break up on Point Loma. Her masts had been pulled out, her once lovely white-painted cabin had been fouled by vandals, and the tide was in her hull.

On the dull, overcast evening of June 17, 1910, San Diegans were puzzled by a series of mournful blasts from a steamer's whistle; it was the American-Hawaiian freighter *Alaskan*, alongside East Santa Fe Wharf—and she was afire in No. 4 and No. 5 holds. Fire apparatus, still for the most part horse-drawn in 1910, clattered down to the wharf and immediately ran into a problem: the *Alaskan's* cargo contained 500 tons of calcium carbide which, if water got to it, would release enough acetylene gas to blow her sky-high. So Fire Chief Louis Almgren tried an alternative strategy; hatches were battened down, ventillators were sealed off with canvas, and everything else was done to cut off any supply of air to the burning cargo.

With hand-drills, holes were bored through her already hot plates and, to get nearer the centers of the two involved holds, up through the top plating of the shaft-alley. Red rubber hose-lines were led down from the chemical tanks which, in those days, every self-respecting hose-wagon carried, and a special call was sent out for "The Medicine-Wagon"—a lovely, copper-tanked Holloway Double-80 of 1898 vintage, which was the city's only chemical-engine. Hopefully, the gas-charged water would settle to the bilges and the heavy carbon dioxide would eventually rise to the level of the fire.

After three days of this treatment the fire was still burning, and San Diego was out of bicarbonate of soda and of sulphuric acid—so American-Hawaiian sent down a carload from Los Angeles. After a week it was found that Los Angeles also was running low on these chemicals—but Almgren had heard of a stock-pile, somewhere, of "drums of liquid carbonic-acid gas" and arranged to get them. The gas went into the hold, and the next time they took off a hatch for inspection, the temperature in the hold had gone down to a mere 80°. After a battle of nearly three weeks the fire was out; some say that it was the first time in fire-fighting history that a shipboard fire was smothered with CO_2, and this may well be true. In a graceful gesture of appreciation, American-Hawaiian threw a big party for the firemen, replaced every damaged uniform, and had the chemical-spattered fire-engines re-painted at the line's own expense.

So much for San Diego's outstanding marine casualties which may be pin-pointed and explained; there were two cases at least which, to this day, remain mysteries. Take, for instance, the British bark *Lizzie Iredale,* which left Newcastle, N.S.W., for San Diego on March 5, 1887, with 1,010 tons of coal; she belonged to the Liverpool firm of Peter Iredale & Sons and was commanded by one of the family, Capt. H. W. Iredale. The voyage should have taken about 60 days, and anxiety developed when this interval was passed by days and then by many weeks. Five months later she was given up as lost, and an inquiry held at Newcastle revealed that she was ". . . strong, staunch and seaworthy in every respect, her Plimsoll disc being four inches clear of the water" when she left for San Diego. What happened? Did her cargo of coal get afire? Did a sudden squall in the night dismast her—or send one of her yards down, end-on, to puncture her deck or smash in a hatch-cover, so that with her heavy cargo she quickly filled and sank? No one will ever know anything more than the bare fact that after clearing Newcastle she was never seen again.

And there was the British bark *Senegal*, Captain Stevens. She came in from Swansea Feb. 17, 1894, discharged her cargo of coal, lay around waiting for a charter and finally left for Puget Sound, in ballast, on the blustery morning of April 15. Subsequently it was learned that, three days later, she was sighted by the little schooner *Mary E. Russ*, just at dusk, and in what the schooner's captain described as "a hard northwesterly gale." She was making heavy weather of it, and in fact the schooner was having her own problems as well. Darkness fell, and at dawn the *Mary E. Russ* was alone on a storm-lashed sea.

Some think that her ballast was improperly stowed or was insufficient, and that she rolled over and sank during the night, but no one will ever know. Her epitaph is grim in its finality, yet tragically frustrating in its vagueness—

> Senegal, *Stevens; British bark, 1389 tons. Left San Diego for Tacoma Apr. 15, 1894, and has not since reported.*

16. Four-score Years of Ferries

My favver, 'e's a fireman, 'e wears a Gor-blime 'at
An' Gor-blime sooty trahsers—now, wot yer fink o' that?
'E wears no blinkin' collar around 'is bloomin' froat,
Coz my old man's a fireman on a ruddy ferryboat!
                              —OLD MUSIC-HALL SONG

Ah, well, *señor;* easy come, easy go. Don Pedro Carrillo had been given the Rancho of the Peninsula of San Diego by his good friend Don Pio Pico, last of the Mexican governors of California, on May 15, 1846. With Yankee occupation looming on the horizon, Don Pio was seeing to it that the right people were taken care of while there was still time. And now, only half a year later, Don Pedro was selling it to Capt. Bezer Simmons of the American ship *Magnolia* for $1,000. Payment, so the story goes, would be in silver; one could not be too careful when dealing with strangers—especially Yankee sea-captains. Remember O'Cain? Shaler? Bradshaw? Por Dios, Señor!

The rancho consisted of Coronado, North Island, and what old-timers called The Sand-Spit, today identified by the more elegant title of The Silver Strand. Simmons kept his real estate for four years and then sold it, some say for $3,000 and others say $10,000. Various owners and would-be owners flitted across the screen and they included William H. Aspinwall of Pacific Mail Steamship fame, and his associate Archibald Peachy, who took over on June 11, 1869. When E. S. Babcock and H. L. Story got it in December of 1885, the price had gone up to $100,000. They incorporated the Coronado Beach Co. in April of 1886 and proceeded to sell lots, from which they made nothing but money. The Beach Company also got busy with a steam street-car line, a shipyard, an iron-works—and, of course, a ferry system across the bay to San Diego. And construction began on that gorgeous monument to untrammeled Victoriana at its best, the Hotel del Coronado.

The first ferryboat was a tiny steam-launch named *Della*, built in Waltham,

---

On the next page: In her final years, the Benicia's *walking-beam was housed over; the reason for this is not clear, nor is the reason why the artist for this tourist picture-book thought that he could draw convincing smoke with a pencil. It is about 1899, and one of the British transpacific freighters is in the distance, at the East Santa Fe Wharf.*—SAN DIEGO PUBLIC LIBRARY

Mass., in 1885, and brought out to San Diego on a flat-car. She was 21 feet long, her official gross tonnage was 2.09, her watch-charm engine was rated at 2 h.p., and on her first trip as a ferry her crew consisted of Captain Babcock and Chief Engineer Story. There were times when the tug *Gen. McPherson* also served as a ferry, with or without a barge-load of raw material for the real-estate agents.

Bigger and better things, however, were in the offing. Alexander Hay, noted San Francisco shipbuilder, was commissioned to design and build a ferryboat and in August of 1886 she arrived—the side-wheeler *Coronado* of 308.54 tons gross, 100 feet long and driven by a single-cylinder inclined engine of 200 indicated horsepower, by Hinkley, Spiers & Hayes. Originally a coal-burner, she was lighted throughout by kerosene lamps—right up to 1920, when she made her last run.

Coronado lots having sold like beer on a hot day, almost at once she was too small. So they had a big one designed by the Union Iron Works at San Francisco, and set up their own shipyard on the north shore of Coronado. At this point some genius decided to improve upon Union's blueprints, so they lengthened the hull by 10 feet, deepened it a foot or so, and instead of the originally designed single-deck superstructure she blossomed out with two decks of Elegant Eighties jig-saw work second only to the Hotel Del itself. They didn't increase her power, and as a result of all that added weight it was hard to get her started—and a great deal harder to get her stopped. The first propeller-driven double-ender on the coast, she was not what one would call a howling success. After a month or so of smashing up the ferry-slips they laid her up; this was in the summer of 1888. Later she became a floating dance-pavillion in Glorietta Bay, and she ended her days as the quarters of the San Diego Yacht Club. A sizeable ferry even by today's standards, the *Silver Gate* was 187 feet long and grossed 528 tons.

Having burned its fingers on home-talent ferry-building, the Beach Company now bought a flat-bottomed side-wheeler named *Benicia,* which had been built at Martinez in 1881, to haul sheep and cattle across the Carquinez Strait. The only San Diego ferry to have a walking-beam engine, she was only 92 feet long and the carriage-way, which curved out to one side and then back again to by-pass the machinery, was open to the sky. She arrived July 18, 1888, and in her hoydenish way became something of a tradition. That curved carriage-way presented problems, and heavy loads had to be carried only at the ends, where the driveway was more or less on the center-line. One day they forgot and spotted a dump-cart full of sand amidships—and hence, far off side. She listed until one paddle-wheel was all but submerged, the other one was out of water, and when she got out of the slip, naturally all that she could do was go around in a circle. Frantic tootling of the whistle brought the *Santa Fe* tug to her assistance, and she was towed home in disgrace.

The engineer, a dour character, was in full view of the occupants of the vehicles she carried, through the engineroom half-door, and one day a timid lady passenger called out from her carriage, as they wallowed across the bay in a south-easter:

"Dear me! Do you think this boat is going down?"

"Madame," he replied, with a sardonic smile, "from the condition of her boiler, I'd be much less surprised if she went up!"

The *Benicia* made her last run on July 4, 1903, and her place was taken immediately by the side-wheeler *Ramona*, which had just arrived from the yard of the Risdon Iron Works on San Francisco Bay. She was 118 feet long with an inclined cross-compound engine, and had the distinction of being the first San Diego Bay vessel to have electric lights. She ran until 1929, and her old age was one of sorrow; used variously as a night-club (which sank from obscure causes) and a fish-boat, after her cabins were torn off; she wound up as a rubbish-barge. She could carry 14 autos, which was enough until 1920, when the larger *Morena* was built. The product of a war-time San Pedro shipyard, she was plain to the point of austerity, and was about as beautiful as one of today's faceless office-buildings—but she was important as the last side-wheeler built in California and the last steam ferry on San Diego Bay; she ran until 1938.

The second *Coronado*, of 1929, brought the steel hull and the Diesel-electric drive to San Diego Bay; she was built, as were the last two ferries, by the Moore Shipbuilding & Drydock Co. in Oakland. At 178 feet she was still 9 feet shorter than the *Silver Gate* of 1888, whose length was not exceeded until the second steel one, the *San Diego*, was launched in 1931. A few years later they bought the former Southern Pacific-Golden Gate Ferries wooden-hulled *Golden West*, altered her extensively and re-named her *North Island;* she was built by James Robertson at Alameda in 1923. Shortly before the Second World War her San Francisco fleet-mate *Golden Shore* (which meanwhile had been the *Elwha* on Puget Sound) joined her, as the *Silver Strand;* she, too, was wooden and came from Alameda, having been built by General Engineering in 1927. The last and largest San Diego-Coronado ferry, the open-deck, steel *Crown City*, capable of handling some 60 automobiles, was built in 1954; her tonnage was 678 and she was 242 feet long.

There were other ferries as well. In 1888 the little steamer *Roseville* was built by Joseph Supple for the Point Loma Land & Town Co., and began daily service from San Diego to Roseville, La Playa and Ballast Point. She ran for a few years and was sold, converted into a tug and sent to some Central American port. She was only 67 feet long—but her little passenger-cabin boasted of plush upholstery and, of all things, a piano. Her purser was, in a small way, a piano-player; his repertoire was limited to one tune, *Listen to the Mocking Bird*, which he loved to play, especially if there were any attractive lady passengers aboard. It finally got on the captain's nerves so badly that he complained to the owners, and as pursers were easier to find than captains, the music ceased.

Now the gasoline engine was coming into its own, and around the turn of the century we find Capt. Bob Baker, while still in high school, bringing Point Loma passengers to San Diego in the morning and taking them home late in the afternoon, in a small launch. The Point Loma Ferry later was served by the Star & Crescent Boat Co.'s much larger *Fortuna, Golden West* and others, and lasted until about 1919, when street-car service from San Diego to Point Loma made it unneccessary. The Army had its own ferry service from Fort Rosecrans (a Coast Artillery post) and San Diego, using the big steam-launch *Gen. De Russy* and the handsome "artillery steamer" *Lieut. Geo. M. Harris*. There also was briefly, in 1910, ferry service from San Diego to Imperial Beach, using the gasoline-driven *Imperial* and *McKinley Jr*. They ran from the old McKinley Boat House at the foot of Market St., up to the head of the bay and into a dredged canal, where they connected with a battery-driven street-car from Imperial Beach.

North Island, meanwhile, had remained an area of sage-brush and jack-rabbits, almost its sole improvement being the Marine Ways. In 1910 Glenn Curtiss obtained the use of some abandoned frame buildings and started a flying school—and in the early part of 1911 made the first successful take-off of a "hydro-aeroplane" from the waters of Spanish Bight, a shallow area (since filled in) which separated North Island from Coronado. His outfit was taken over by the Army Signal Corps—which handled the service's flying until the Army Air Corps took over about the time of the First World War—and it became Rockwell Field. That was in 1912, and now the Navy was getting increasingly air-minded. On Aug. 1, 1917, the first land for the Naval Air Station was acquired, and the following month occupancy of some existing buildings was authorized. When Rockwell Field was phased out some years later the Navy expanded greatly, and Star & Crescent set up the North Island Ferry. At first they used the *Golden West* and *Virginia*, then they built the *Scout* and the *Hyack*, and eventually a fleet of flat-bottom, square-ended Diesel ferries—actually self-propelled passenger-scows —of good capacity and a fair turn of speed; these included the *Juanita, Del Mar, Glorietta* and *Monterey*. Affectionately dubbed the "Nickle-Snatcher" ferry, it handled thousands of commuters daily at 5 cents a passenger. Many years passed before the owners, faced by steadily rising operating costs, reluctantly went to a 10-cent fare.

17. Era of Concrete and Steel

The Port of San Diego provides modern marine terminals with rapid cargo-handling facilities and equipment; 37 feet is maintained alongside the piers and docks.

— *U. S. Coast Pilot 7, Pacific Coast* (1963)

On June 6, 1919, the barkentine *Benicia,* Puget Sound for Cape Town with lumber, put in at San Diego, but not because she wanted to; she was having trouble with her caulking and with her sailors. Both problems eventually were resolved and she went on about her business. Why is she mentioned here? Because she marked the end of an era, in a year when other eras began or ended: She was the last sailing-vessel, with cargo, to visit San Diego Bay. "Ah," you may say, "but what of the full-rigged ships *Indiana* and *Bohemia,* and the four-masted schooner *Lottie Bennett?*" True, the two old Down Easters called briefly in the late 1920s, but they were in ballast—and in the movies; the schooner, which came in some ten years later, had by then acquired a Diesel engine, which cancelled her status as a pure windjammer. She came in under power.

San Diego's harbor development had been, for many years, a bit on the informal side, and there is little doubt but what this was due, to an appreciable extent, to the fact that the harbor was run from Sacramento rather than locally. The Federal government had whittled away at Middleground Shoal and built the jetty and deepened the channel across the bar, but that was about all. Finally, in 1911, the State of California grudgingly relinquished control of the tidelands to the city—on condition that the city would raise $1,000,000 through a bond election for port development. The next year San Diego fooled Sacramento by doing just that, and in 1914 they voted

---

On the next page: The San Diego-Coronado bridge nears completion—and with its opening, 83 years of ferryboat operation on the bay will pass into history. Coronado having previously rejected schemes for a bridge, its building has not been without some controversy.—COURTESY OF UNION-TRIBUNE PUBLISHING CO.

another $400,000. A 30-foot channel was dredged in to the foot of Broadway, and they built the 800-foot Broadway Pier with its corrugated-iron pier shed, and offices at the inboard end; it was San Diego's first reinforced-concrete pier. The gasoline-powered suction-dredge *E. M. Capps*, appropriately named for the engineer who planned the whole project, was popularly supposed to be the first suction-dredge on the bay, which of course it was not. They had used a steam suction-dredge in Glorietta Bay, on the Coronado side, away back in 1888, and shortly after the turn of the century the suction-dredge *Salt Lake City* had worked on Middleground Shoal and on the bar.

Early in 1918 Joe Brennan, of tugboat fame, was named Harbor Master and a few years later what he called "an Irish promotion—a fancier name but no more pay," changed his title to Port Director. And in 1919, the year which saw the little barkentine come and go, the first Harbor Commission, of three men, was appointed by the mayor. When Brennan retired in 1948 he could look back on the passing of the last wooden cargo wharves, building the 1,000-foot B Street Pier, lengthening Broadway Pier to 1,000 feet and double-decking it—and creating Lindbergh Field, the municipal airport.

It was also in 1919 that the city gave the Navy 79 acres of submerged tidelands in the Dutch Flats area just north of the main channel in from Point Loma, and raised the funds to buy 135 acres of privately owned adjacent land to go with it. The Corps of Engineers of the U. S. Army moved the bulkhead line out to what had been set as the pierhead line, providing a big area into which to pump mud from the bottom of the bay as the deep-water areas were extended. Development was not easy; voters tended to be bond-shy, and before they got the needed $1,000,000 for B Street Pier, built in 1926, they had to break it up into thirds, and go after them one at a time.

John Bate was named to succeed Brennan as Port Director, and he took to the job with great vigor and vision. In his drive for a bigger and better port, with an increasing stream of outward as well as inward cargo, the air was not always free from sparks; one local writer hung on him the nickname of "The Terrible-Tempered Mr. Bate", an appropriate designation when he crossed swords with people unsympathetic toward harbor development. He led the drive for the huge Tenth Avenue Marine Terminal and it is interesting to note that while the voters had boggled at a $1,000,000 bond-issue for B Street Pier in 1926, they cheerfully voted $9,460,000 for Tenth Avenue in 1955. The terminal was opened in 1958 and its equipment includes four huge transit-sheds, a bulk-loader capable of handling 2,000 tons an hour—and dockside bunkering facilities.

Legislation permitting the cities of San Diego, National City, Chula Vista, Coronado and Imperial Beach to join in a Unified Port District was passed by the State Legislature in 1962, and the Harbor Commission was replaced by a seven-man Board of Port Commissioners—three from San Diego and one apiece from each of the smaller cities. Their first job was the formulation of a Master Plan for port development, which after public hearings was adopted in 1964. In that same year the Marketing Operations Department was set up to develop tonnage through the port, and the voters approved a $10,870,000 expenditure in three bond issues for future port development.

The business of a port is to handle ships and cargo, but for many years due thought has been given to the recreational and other needs of the community. Ever since the 1880s there have been yacht clubs and rowing clubs, frequently forced to move as commercial needs crowded them out, but for many years scant attention was given to public small-craft and other recreational facilities. And then, men with imagination began looking at a big, useless mud-flat paralleling Point Loma on its bay side.

In 1934, it was decided that this mud-flat would be a good place to dump the spoil from a channel-deepening project and to create, between it and the shoreline, a yacht basin. Today that mud-flat is Shelter Island, a vista of palm-trees, motels, green lawns, restaurants, ship-chandlers and all the rest, right in the area where Pacific Mail's lumbering side-wheelers used to take coal from the pathetic old *Clarissa Andrews* a century and more ago. The "forest of spars" of the old days of Babcock & Story's Wharf is repeated—in smaller units but with astronomically more of them—by hundreds of yachts in the basin which lies inshore of Shelter Island.

Harbor Island, the new recreational area on the north side of the channel, is what might be called a fringe-benefit from Navy dredging. In order to get the big new aircraft carriers of the *Forrestal* class alongside the quay at North Island without complications, they needed 42 feet of water in the area and there had to be some place to dump the mud which was dredged up. So they ran a submerged pipeline across the channel, and through it they filled in what became Harbor Island.

The 1964 bond issue provided for the completion of Harbor Island, putting up a huge new airport terminal building, and creating the Twenty-fourth Street terminal at National City—which is in hailing distance of the site of Kimball's wharf of the 1880s. It was in use even before its formal opening late in 1968, and in the first three months of its operation it handled 26 ocean-going barges, a scrap-metal ship, 13 tankers and eight miscellaneous vessels; over it moved 40,000,000 board-feet of lumber, 11,500 tons of scrap metal, 388,000 barrels of oil and 510 tons of oil waste. Final stages of the creation of Harbor Island added, in 1967, another place-name to San Diego Bay, Spanish Landing. No Spaniard ever landed there, of course, because the whole area was under water in those century-past Spanish days, but the name is of interest as suggesting the built-in peril of selecting place-names by a popular contest.

In 1964 John Bate retired as Port Director and was succeeded by Don L. Nay, his chief assistant; it was only the second change of directors in half a century, which may give a hint as to why port development in San Diego has gone along so effectively. The physical changes during that period, however, have been spectacular. Piers now are of concrete and steel instead of fire-tempting creosoted fir; steamers and motorships can bunker at the same berth where they load or lay down cargo, and the whine of the electric winch has replaced the tramp, tramp, tramp of heavy boots around the capstan. The tall funnel of the coal-burner has joined the tall masts of the Cape Horner in oblivion, and instead of sage-brush it is radar antennae which crown Point Loma, as they crown the exotic types of warcraft which have replaced the torpedoboat and the monitor. Water-borne passengers now come to San Diego only by sporadic cruise-ships—but air-borne travelers handled through the port are about 3,000,000 a year. The only visible link with a lusty past is the century-old bark *Star of India,* rescued from the imminent threat of the knacker's torch and now, restored as a maritime museum, one of San Diego's better tourist attractions. Once in a while she has company when a square-rigged training-ship makes port, but they all have auxiliary Diesels, and no doubt the little old Iron Lady looks down her forestay at them.

A lot of people have played their major or minor parts in the making of this rather impressive port, and many of them have passed on to Fiddlers' Green. The bewhiskered crews of the little steam pile-drivers and clam-shell dredges have given way to today's hard-hatted construction workers and the solemn young men with slide-rules sticking out of their pockets. Gone is the pig-tailed Chinese fisherman in his picturesque junk, and the longshoreman shovelling sand-ballast or coal to earn a dollar or so a day which, that night, probably would be left in some bistro in Stingaree. And gone as well is another vanished type who got to San Diego from the far ports of the world by his own brawn and skill and courage—the lean, tough, hard-fisted Cape Horn sailorman.

To all of these men is the modern Port of San Diego indebted—masters and fo'csl hands, pilots and dock-wallopers, engineers and donkey-men— who have earned a valediction like Conrad's unforgettable farewell to the crew of the *Narcissus:*

> ".... *You were a good crowd. As good a crowd as ever fisted with wild cries the beating canvas of a heavy foresail; or tossing aloft, invisible in the night, gave back yell for yell to a westerly gale.*"

Years of patient study and countless hours of superb craftsmanship are represented in this scale model of the brig Pilgrim, *in which Richard Henry Dana first came to San Diego, in the lusty days of the hide-ships.*

— SAN FRANCISCO MARITIME MUSEUM

Under a late afternoon "high fog" Maj. John C. Fremont's troops leave the Cyane *to secure newly-acquired San Diego. It is obvious that a lot of research went into this historic painting, done by Carlton T. Chapman in 1913. Between the* Cyane *and Point Loma lies the Mexican brig* Juanita, *while just above the troop-laden boats appear the Yankee hide-houses at La Playa; the date is July 29, 1846. Contrary to popular (and even published) accounts, this was not the same* Cyane *which was captured by the U.S.S.* Constitution *from the British in 1815. San Diego's* Cyane *was built at Boston Navy Yard in 1837, decommissioned at Mare Island in 1871, and sold at auction July 30, 1887.*

— COLLECTION OF JOSEPH E. JESSOP

First of the big Cape Horners to visit San Diego was the handsome four-masted ship Trafalgar, *of Glasgow; she arrived in the summer of 1881 and is seen here, her cargo discharged, lying at anchor, with brush-covered Coronado in the background. Built by Connell, of Glasgow, in 1877, she lasted until Nov. 19, 1904, when she was wrecked while on a passage from Sydney, N.S.W., toward Falmouth.*

— HISTORICAL COLLECTION,
TITLE INSURANCE & TRUST CO.

The all-time record of 112 days from New York to San Diego was set by the clipper ship Stillwell S. Bishop *in 1853 and it would be another 28 years before the second one from New York arrived. This time it was the bark* James A. Wright, *shown here at a San Francisco wharf, and she came in to San Diego Bay Sept. 8, 1881, having taken 147 days to do it. Her cargo, which she unloaded at National City, was significant, for it contained three locomotives for San Diego's first railroad.*

— SAN FRANCISCO MARITIME MUSEUM

Lower yards were commonly used for cargo-booms, as this 1888 view at National City Wharf shows. The three British Cape Horners are the Moel-y-Don, Mirzapore *(in background) and* Duke of Argyll. *All are discharging coal.*

— HISTORICAL COLLECTION,
TITLE INSURANCE & TRUST CO.

It was down around Sunda Strait in 1863 that the American ship Belvedere *made history by out-running the Confederate raider* Alabama, *and that is why it was possible for her to pose for her photo in San Diego Bay in the summer of 1886. She is loading ballast through a side-port, and off her starboard quarter lies the steam tug* Emma, *the first locally-built steamer. It was the* Belvedere's *last portrait; three months later, on Nov. 29, 1886, she blundered onto Vancouver Island in a pea-soup fog, and the seas made short work of her.*

— HISTORICAL COLLECTION,
TITLE INSURANCE & TRUST CO.

Two handsome Down Easters, relegated to the West Coast coal trade, at National City Wharf in the early Eighties. At the left is the Valley Forge, which once sailed into San Diego Bay with a full load of coal but no tug; to the right is the main-skys'l-yarder Shirley. The little wood-burning locomotive, California Southern's Three Spot, also could claim Cape Horn status, having come out from New York in the hold of the James A. Wright.

— HISTORICAL COLLECTION,
TITLE INSURANCE & TRUST CO.

A link with maritime literature. The little schooner Jennie Thelin, whose past was not always exemplary, was the one Jack London had in mind when he wrote of the schooner Ghost, in "The Sea Wolf". Built at Davenport Landing, she operated originally in the far north, but ended her days in the prosaic guano trade, out of San Diego; she was lost on the Lower Coast in 1913.

— CAPT. JOE BRENNAN COLLECTION

Apparently both captains decided that it was time to paint the yards, as indicated by the dropping of the snugly furled sails on the barkentines Retriever (left) and Malay. The location is Babcock & Story's Wharf, the year is 1887 and the little steamer whose masts and funnel just show above a pile of lumber is the Mexican coaster Manuel Dublan.

— SAN FRANCISCO MARITIME MUSEUM

Stuns'l booms were a rarity by 1905 — but there is no mistaking them, on the fore-yard of the survey-ship Galilee; what is more, Captain Hayes set his stuns'ls and gave San Diego waterfronters a real thrill as he came triumphantly up the bay from off La Playa, on Dec. 9 of that year. The trim little hermaphrodite brig, then doing oceanographic work for the Carnegie Institute, later became a three-masted schooner, in the fisheries trade.

— HISTORICAL COLLECTION,
TITLE INSURANCE & TRUST CO.

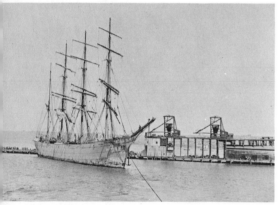

A jingle and one bell — "Ahead, dead slow" — and the tow-line becomes taut. More bells, and the German four-masted bark Omega swings out and away from Coal Bunkers Wharf in the summer of 1910, bound for the open sea. She was the old Drumcliff and she lasted until 1958, when a long and useful life was ended by a rock on the Peruvian coast.

— CAPT. JOE BRENNAN COLLECTION

There were those who said that the Pass of Melfort was the most handsome ship ever to visit San Diego. The big British four-masted bark came in twice, from Newcastle, N.S.W. in 1892 and from Hamburg almost exactly ten years later. She was wrecked near the entrance to Barclay Sound in the winter of 1905, while coming up from South America. There were no survivors.

— JAY COOKE

Even after tugs became available, frugal square-rigger captains occasionally would beat down the bay to Point Loma under jibs and stays'ls, setting the square stuff as they began to head off the wind. This view of around 1895 is from North Island, looking across the channel to the west. The little bark just passing the lighthouse is unidentified, but it could be the Vidette.

— HISTORICAL COLLECTION,
TITLE INSURANCE & TRUST CO.

Her cargo discharged, the schooner Irene is outward bound in this photo of around 1910, under the skillful direction of Capt. S. C. Mitchell, who looked down his nose at tugs, and prided himself on getting in and out under sail. Today the bare hills behind her are all but solid with houses.

— HISTORICAL COLLECTION,
TITLE INSURANCE & TRUST CO.

A frequent visitor was the trim, three-masted schooner Halcyon, and she set the record of 9½ days from Seabeck, Washington Territory, to San Diego. Here she lies at the Fifth Street Wharf about 1890, in company with the passenger steamer George W. Elder.

— HISTORICAL COLLECTION,
TITLE INSURANCE & TRUST CO.

West Santa Fe Wharf was a busy place in the spring of 1888. The bark James A. Borland (it was shortened to "J. A." on her transom) lies stern to camera and across the wharf from her is the British steamer Montserrat, which went missing from Nanaimo, B.C., in '94. Aside from the steam tug Gen. McPherson and the ferryboat Silver Gate, whose pilot-house is just behind that piledriver, the rest are unidentified.

— HISTORICAL COLLECTION,
TITLE INSURANCE & TRUST CO.

The end of a glorious era: the three-skys'l-yarder Aryan *arriving off San Diego in 1910. She was the last full-rigged ship built in America and on her long voyage out from Philadelphia her captain had suffered a stroke, sails had been blown out of the bolt-ropes — and her cargo of coal had been on fire.*

— HISTORICAL COLLECTION,
TITLE INSURANCE & TRUST CO.

Trading to the Lower Coast — fishing — sealing — poaching — smuggling; you name it and at one time or another it would fit the schooner Lou, perhaps the most colorful of the Mosquito Fleet. Her origin is obscure, but she was rebuilt at San Diego in 1883 from a big sloop called Newhope which, so the story goes, came around Cape Horn in 1850. There is a legend that in San Francisco, at the time of one of the waterfront executions, the Vigilance Committee's hangman requisitioned her jib-halliard for that day's grim business. Here she is shown beached at the foot of H (now Market) Street in 1909.

— HISTORICAL COLLECTION,
TITLE INSURANCE & TRUST CO.

The only one of that little group of steel sailing vessels built in the United States ever to visit San Diego, the four-masted bark Acme *was towed in on the morning of April 23, 1910. Her time of 125 days from Philadelphia was the best ever logged for that run; the average was 169. Just astern of her on Point Loma is the U. S. Quarantine Station and wharf, now a part of the Naval Electronics Laboratory. Later the* Star of Poland, *she was lost in 1918.*

— CAPT. JOE BRENNAN COLLECTION

Ah, name of a thousand peegs! Ze ruddaire, he is make squeaky noise! So they have shifted ballast to get her stern up, one man is down on a jacobs-ladder and two more are out in one of her boats, to see what ails the steering-gear of the French bark Amiral de Cornulier. *The year is 1907 and the timber truss in the foreground is part of the pontoon bridge for the Coronado ferry slip.*

— HISTORICAL COLLECTION,
TITLE INSURANCE & TRUST CO.

The "jubilee-rigged" British ship Dudhope, *last of the Cape Horners to make San Diego, is picked up by the tug, on Nov. 30, 1914. The not-so-handsome rig — double top-gallants and no royals — gets its unusual name from the fact that it came out in 1887, the year of Queen Victoria's Golden Jubilee.*

— HISTORICAL COLLECTION,
TITLE INSURANCE & TRUST CO.

The Russian bark California, *when within about 200 miles of San Diego late in 1911, ran into a gale and lost her main royal-mast, as the snapshot shows. Here she lies off North Island, taking ballast.*

— PHOTO BY AUTHOR

Did they run out of grey paint? Or did the job of chipping and red-leading her plates take longer than was anticipated? At any rate, the Hera, *of Hamburg, presented a rather informal appearance when she left San Diego in 1910.*

— CAPT. JOE BRENNAN COLLECTION

Men Against the Sea — and men against the rust. Under the graceful bow of the French full-rigged ship Desaix, a group of her sailors is busy with chipping-hammers and pots of red-lead, carrying on the battle against corrosion which, in a steel ship, is never more than a delaying action. She's at the East Santa Fe Wharf, it is autumn of 1914 and in the hazy distance are North Island and Point Loma.

— BOB NEILL

An occasional visitor to San Diego was the topsail-schooner Americana, shown here hauled out on the marine railway at North Island in 1903. A steel vessel of 839 tons, she was built at Grangemouth, Scotland, in 1892. On Feb. 28, 1918, she sailed from Astoria, Ore., and was never seen again.

— HISTORICAL COLLECTION,
TITLE INSURANCE & TRUST CO.

San Diego's Civic Center, now the County Administration Center, seen under the bowsprit of the four-masted schooner Lottie Bennett in 1938 — and where today would you find someone who could carve those lovely acanthus-leaves on her trail-board?

— PHOTO BY AUTHOR

With a clam-shell bucket, Spreckels Brothers' derrick-barge is loading ballast into the German four-masted bark Lisbeth, off the Coal Bunkers in the summer of 1909. Anchored further up-stream is the handsome Belfast ship G. W. Wolff.

— HISTORICAL COLLECTION,
TITLE INSURANCE & TRUST CO.

In her old age a lot of unpleasant things happened to the once handsome schooner Mary Dodge — like sawing off her jibboom and installing an auxiliary engine. Here she is, bound for the Lower Coast in 1915, with a deckload of hay that would make the skipper of a Sacramento River scow-schooner green with envy.

— CAPT. JOE BRENNAN COLLECTION

And now the wind has hauled to the nor'west and the storm is breaking up; tomorrow will be clear and cold. Aboard the little trading-schooner Ellen Capt. Roelf Oosterhuis (well-known around Batavia before he came to San Diego) is drying out gear and in a few minutes they will be making Evening Colors aboard the U. S. S. Chicago, lying stern-to-camera in this 1905 view.

— HISTORICAL COLLECTION,
TITLE INSURANCE & TRUST CO.

Just heeling slightly to a gentle afternoon breeze, the veteran Japanese training-bark Taisei Maru passes out from San Diego Bay, around 1930. Everything is sheeted home, and they're about to secure the boiler for her little auxiliary steam engine.

— PHOTO BY AUTHOR

One of the very few four-masted steel barks ever built in this country, the Erskine M. Phelps became a Union Oil tank-barge, and is seen here, unloading at Coronado around 1914. Built by the Sewalls at Bath, Mo., in 1898, her hull and cabins were in mint condition when the government took her over during the Second World War and sent her off to the South Pacific as the YON-147. After the war San Francisco wanted her for historic restoration — only to find that, instead of towing her home, they had scuttled her at Manus on Dec. 8, 1945.

— FRED REIF COLLECTION.

It's early afternoon of a crisp autumn day —
Oct. 11, 1911 — and the barkentine S. N.
Castle *has come in on the flood tide, 47 days
from the Tuamotus with a load of phosphate
rock; the little* Santa Fe *is nosing her in to a
berth at Spreckels Wharf. Built by Hall Bros.
at Port Blakeley in 1886, the trim skys'l-
yarder "went Hollywood" in her old age,
and was blown up in the production of that
excellent silent film,* Old Ironsides.

— HISTORICAL COLLECTION,
TITLE INSURANCE & TRUST CO.

*Before she finally settled to the bottom, the
handsome little* Galilee *served as an artist's
home in Sausalito. In the background is the
hulk of the big four-masted schooner* Commerce; *the time is 1943.*

— PHOTO BY AUTHOR

*Among the vessels whose portraits were done
by the mysterious Joseph Lee was the little*
Mary E. Russ *of 1875, which in her time
brought enough redwood to San Diego to
build a fair part of the growing town — and
was the last vessel to sight the British bark*
Senegal, *which went missing in 1894 while
on a passage from San Diego for Tacoma.*

— COLLECTION OF KENNETH CLYDE JENKINS

*Most of San Diego's early houses were built
of redwood, brought in by small schooners
from the "dog-holes" of the Mendocino coast.
This wood-engraving from an old school
geography shows how the lumber was slid
down a chute from the cliffs, to a schooner
secured by four mooring-lines.*

— DON M. STEWART COLLECTION

Even in light airs, those soft, gray sails of hempen canvas set without a wrinkle. The steel, four-masted bark Nippon Maru, training cadets from the Royal Nautical College of Kobe, prepares to pick up her pilot at San Diego, in the late 1930s.

— PHOTO BY AUTHOR

Lashed down into place, the two "harness-casks" — one for salt beef, one for salt pork — are seen at the break of the poop; between them the portable "cow bridge" from the poop to the standard compass platform on the after boat-skids has been raised, to give access to the mizzen hatch. A photographer took advantage of a splatter of rain which drove ship's officers, and visitors, under shelter as the French ship David d'Angers unloaded at the Coal Bunkers in the winter of 1910.

— CAPT. JOE BRENNAN COLLECTION

There's a lively connotation to the word "Quickstep" — and the barkentine Quickstep lived up to it, all through her life. Her San Diego cargoes always were lumber from the Pacific Northwest, including much of the heavy framing for the Hotel del Coronado. But she traded elsewhere, too, and on one voyage Capt. George J. Fake brought her from New York to Portland, Ore., in the excellent time of 128 days. The Halls built her, at Port Ludlow in 1876, and this is her "portrait", by the famous Joseph Lee.

COURTESY COMDR. F. B. FAKE U.S.N. (RET.)

For many years the barkentine Modoc visited San Diego and National City, generally with half a million feet of lumber from Puget Sound. She was built at Utsalady, Washington Territory, in 1873, by the famous ship-builder George Boole. This painting, by W. A. Coulter, shows her winning the Master Mariners' Race at San Francisco, July 4, 1879.

— COURTESY OF MRS. S. T. JOHNSON

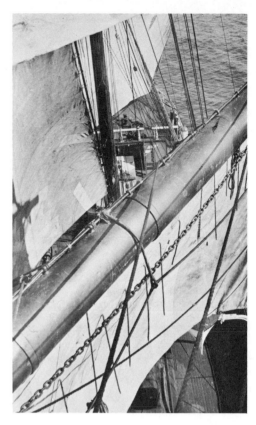

A nostalgic link with San Diego's Glory Days of Sail — the veteran bark Star of India at the Embarcadero, just north of B Street Pier. Launched at Ramsey, Isle of Man, in 1863, she originally was the British full-rigged ship Euterpe, and for many years carried passengers and cargo to New Zealand and Australia before obtaining American registry and joining the Alsaka Packers' fleet, of San Francisco. This 1967 view shows her as restored by the Maritime Museum Association of San Diego.

— PHOTO BY AUTHOR

A study in steel and canvas. The view is from the maintop of the Pacific Queen, on her Long Beach-San Diego voyage in the summer of 1935.

— PHOTO BY AUTHOR

Shortly after Old Ironsides — the U. S. S. Constitution — arrived early in January of 1933, they brought the venerable Star of India over to Broadway Pier to keep her company; the frigate's men are laying aloft for an exhibition sail drill. Between the two is the minesweeper Grebe, which towed the Constitution, and just off the Pier Quaker Line's freighter San Bernardino is straightening herself out for the run down-channel.

— LEE PASSMORE

In this spirited 1874 lithograph of San Diego, the mountains have been moved right up to the edge of town — and don't you think it really looks better that way? The canopied wharf in the center of the picture is Culverwell's; Horton's Wharf is at the far right. The somewhat fanciful sidewheeler (Gad! Look where they've put the gallows-frame for her walkingbeam!) is headed right for the mud-flats and will be aground in another 30 seconds or so.

— HISTORICAL COLLECTION,
TITLE INSURANCE & TRUST CO.

Every stick of lumber in the famous Hotel del Coronado — "The Grand Old Lady Who Sits By The Sea" — came into San Diego Bay in sailing vessels, from little two-masted schooners to full-rigged ships. This unusual view of the hotel is from the Worden Collection, and was taken in 1905.

— WELLS FARGO BANK HISTORY ROOM,
SAN FRANCISCO

Early days of San Diego's shipbuilding industry, with a squatter's shack and a bath-house, on Atlantic Street (now Pacific Highway and two blocks inland) at about the foot of D Street (now Broadway). Probably about 1880.

— HISTORICAL COLLECTION,
TITLE INSURANCE & TRUST CO.

Roseville Wharf in 1888, when the only reliable communication between San Diego and Point Loma was by boat. The large building at the left is the old nail-factory, the only thing accomplished in a grandiose scheme for steel mills which, the promoters hoped, would make San Diego "The Pittsburgh of the West." Happily, the plan collapsed with the end of "The Great Boom".

— TURRILL COLLECTION; SOCIETY OF
CALIFORNIA PIONEERS, SAN FRANCISCO

Jorres'—formerly Culverwell's—Wharf at the foot of F Street, in the early 1880s. The man standing in front of the little office-building is William Jorres, who had a tug and a water-barge, and supplied ballast and fresh water to outward-bound sailing vessels. At the right is the warehouse of A. Wentscher — commission agent, German Consul, and operator of a fleet of sloops and small schooners in the Lower Coast trade.

— COURTESY OF DON NEAL EMERSON

Looking across the bay toward Coronado from the Russ Lumber Yard, about 1887. The little diamond-stack 0-4-0 locomotive is California Southern's "Three Spot" and just above her is the hermaphrodite-brig North Star. The bark at the extreme left is the Vidette; the schooners are unidentified.

— HISTORICAL COLLECTION,
TITLE INSURANCE & TRUST CO.

Cable-cars, drawn by a steam engine at the outboard end, carried the coal from the two unloading-chutes in the center of the picture and dumped it into the cavernous, heavily-timbered individual bunkers. In this view of the 1890s, two ships and a bark are discharging at Spreckels' Wharf.

— HISTORICAL COLLECTION,
TITLE INSURANCE & TRUST CO.

The "South Front" in 1914, as seen from the fore upper-topgallant yard of the British ship Dudhope. At lower right is the West Santa Fe Wharf with, above it, the East Santa Fe Wharf and a little further on, wharves of the Pacific Coast Steamship Co. and San Diego Lumber Co. The Star Boat House is at lower left and most of the central, wharf-encircled area, now is filled in.

— PHOTO BY AUTHOR

Soft-coal smoke billows away from the monitor Wyoming, later the Cheyenne, in this early 1900s view; inboard of her lies the Fish Commission's steamer Albatross. The gray building, far right, is the office of the Spreckels Bros. Commercial Co. Just below it in the picture, the schooner Lou, of sometimes dubious repute, reclines in the mud. And below her an industrious Chinese is "tramping bait" — stomping to bring up the crawfish.

— HISTORICAL COLLECTION,
TITLE INSURANCE & TRUST CO.

Low tide at the Coal Bunkers, late on a January afternoon in 1912. In the left foreground is Spreckels' tug Santa Fe, *with the* Bahada *at the far right. The Russian bark* California —*still minus her main royale-mast, has hauled out into the stream to save wharfage.*

— PHOTO BY AUTHOR

Looking down along the north side of B Street Pier; in the distance are the Civic Center (now the County Administration Center) and the steam schooners Barbara Olson *and* Daisy Gray. *At the right is the* Samoa, *whose captain, Nils Sinnes, outsmarted a Japanese submarine off the Northern California coast late in December of 1941, and thereby saved his ship.*

— FRED REIF COLLECTION

Looking south along the crest of Point Loma in 1917. The Quarantine Station is at the left, then the Navy Coaling Station, which by then had been completed. Between it and distant Ballast Point, three coal-barges and a target-raft are anchored; across the channel is the tip of North Island, showing Whalers' Bight, and the low mountains of Mexico appear dimly on the horizon.

— HISTORICAL COLLECTION,
TITLE INSURANCE & TRUST CO.

Cranes are replacing cargo-booms, the "engines aft" freighter is the coming thing, and San Diego's wooden wharves are but a dimming memory. In this aerial view of 1967, going clockwise from the tip of the massive Tenth Avenue terminal are the Norwegian motorship Balto, *States Line's* California, *the Japanese* Sanuki Maru, *American President's steamer* President Lincoln *and around the corner, the Liberian freighter* Oriental Jade. *Across the channel are Coronado and North Island, to the far right is the lower part of San Diego and in the foreground is the bulk-loader.*

— SAN DIEGO UNIFIED PORT DISTRICT

"*The* Santa Fe *tug*" *at the Coal Bunkers in 1911. One of the few twin-screw tugs on the coast, Chris Telson built her at Coronado in 1888, and her machinery came all the way from the Chilicothe Iron Works in Ohio. She had a pair of single-cylinder, oscillating engines mounted on an A-frame, and was non-condensing. Later cut down to a water-barge, she was abandoned around 1920.*

— PHOTO BY AUTHOR

Within the scope of this 1907 aerial photo, Pacific Mail's lumbering sidewheelers called a century ago, to discharge passengers and take on fuel from the coal-hulk Clarissa Andrews; *here Richard Henry Dana landed — and the* Lelia Byrd *thumbed her nose at the Spanish Army. You are looking south-westerly, down the axis of man-made Shelter Island with its hundreds of yachts. Just beyond are the piers where oceanographic vessels of the Naval Alectronics Laboratory, and the University of California, tie up, and the pier and tankfarm of the Navy Fuel Annex. And beyond is Point Loma.*

— SAN DIEGO UNIFIED PORT DISTRICT

San Diego's only tug to boast the traditional gilded eagle atop her pilothouse; the Gen. McPherson, *in the early 1890s. A former Army steamer, she was built in San Francisco in 1867 and came south during the boom. Later she was converted into a two-masted schooner, and left San Diego for Alaskan service in 1898. Alongside Spreckels' Coal Bunkers, to the right, is the British collier* Hounslow.

— HISTORICAL COLLECTION,
TITLE INSURANCE & TRUST CO.

Salt-water house-moving. Early in the century, several homes were moved from Coronado to San Diego for their jittery owners, after a severe storm ate away most of Ocean Boulevard, in those days unprotected by a rock fill. Over at Spreckels Wharf a handsome skys'l-yard bark — an obvious Down Easter — is discharging cargo.

— HISTORICAL COLLECTION,
TITLE INSURANCE & TRUST CO.

The steel tug Bahada *was built by Moran at Seattle in 1902, for the Spreckels Brothers' Commercial Co. and they kept her until the First World War, when she was sold to the Hercules Powder Co., for towing kelp barges. Then she went to San Pedro and eventually returned to her birthplace, Puget Sound — where she was lost with all hands Nov. 21, 1926.*

— CAPT. JOE BRENNAN COLLECTION

Towing a 900-foot log-raft from the Columbia River, the Red Stack tug Hercules *comes in past Point Loma, about 1910.*

— CAPT. JOE BRENNAN COLLECTION

Now the Hercules *has got her ungainly raft of logs safely into the harbor; she has slackened speed and has reeled in most of her towing-wire, for Benson's mill is only a mile away. One of American-Hawaiian's freighters is off her port bow, and the ferryboat* Ramona *is scurrying out of the way.*

— CAPT. JOE BRENNAN COLLECTION

Strength in repose; Red Stack's big steam tug Sea Lion *has just brought a 900-foot raft of logs down from the Columbia, and is taking on fresh water at B Street Pier in the summer of 1938. Capt. Max Jahn is ashore on some last-minute business but he'll be back soon, for in an hour she heads back for her home port of San Francisco.*

— PHOTO BY AUTHOR

When the Bahada took out the German four-masted bark Hera in 1909, members of the local German colony were invited to go along. Upper deck, far left, is Capt. A. A. (Bob) Morris, veteran San Diego tug captain and pilot, and later "commodore" of the Wilmington Transportation Co.'s little fleet of Catalina steamers. Directly below him is Joe Brennan, then the tug's mate-deckhand; by the fire-room door is Jack Telson, engineer, and son of the veteran boatbuilder Chris Telson.

— CAPT. JOE BRENNAN COLLECTION

The 10 a.m. Harbor Excursion is about to leave in the Estrella, in this view from Broadway Pier around 1920; like her fleet-mates Crescent and Virginia, she doubled in the "nickle-snatcher" ferry service to North Island. The gaunt two-story building to the right, since demolished to make way for Navy Pier, had to do with the salt-water intake for cooling the condensers of the power station at Kettner and Broadway. In the distance, just above the words "People's Fish", is historic San Diego Barracks, built in 1850 and torn down in 1921; a seven-story Navy warehouse has replaced the mission-style fish houses.

— HISTORICAL COLLECTION, TITLE INSURANCE & TRUST CO.

Before the mechanized purse-seiner took over, tuna fishing by the hook-and-line method could be a hairy business. This San Diego tunaboat obviously is on a school of "three-pole" tuna — fish so big that it took the combined strength of three brawny men to swing one aboard. If you ever heard of team-work — this was it!

— FRED REIF COLLECTION

In the early Eighties, the federal government ran the whalemen off of Ballast Point; coast defense fortifications for the area were on the drawing-board. So Capt. Enos Wall set up his try-pots and the other gear for a modest whaling station across the channel, on North Island. This view, from a tourist picturebook lithographed in Germany, shows a whale being cut up, with chunks of blubber in the foreground. Point Loma is in the distance.

— HISTORICAL COLLECTION,
TITLE INSURANCE & TRUST CO.

Chinese fishermen were an important if controversial element in San Diego's early days; they dragged tons of pompano from the bay and outside they caught sheep's-head, which they dried in the sun at La Playa and shipped to China. Here are eight of the locally-built Chinese junks — redwood planked — off the foot of Fifth Street about 1887.

— HISTORICAL COLLECTION,
TITLE INSURANCE & TRUST CO.

Joseph Supple (second from left, in white shirt) probably lost that shirt with everything else when The Great Boom became The Great Bust in the late 1880s. Undismayed, he moved to Portland, Ore., to become a highly successful shipbuilder. Here is his shop near the foot of E Street, with the tracks of the California Southern practically underfoot. As a result of filling, the locale now is about two blocks inland.

— HISTORICAL COLLECTION,
TITLE INSURANCE & TRUST CO.

High seas tuna boats at the Campbell Machine Co. for maintenance and repairs, around 1930. During the Second World War many of San Diego's tuna fleet served in the Navy as patrol craft and supply vessels in the South Pacific, and some were lost by enemy action.

— HISTORICAL COLLECTION,
TITLE INSURANCE & TRUST CO.

The San Diego Marine Construction Co., at the foot of Samson Street, in the late 1920s. The largest of the boats hauled out is Guy Silva's Emma R. S., first tuna boat with wireless, with all-electric auxiliaries — and with a small plane for fish-scouting.

— HISTORICAL COLLECTION,
TITLE INSURANCE & TRUST CO.

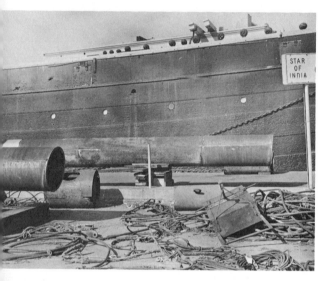

When new sections had to be welded onto the rust-wasted masts of the old Star of India in 1961, San Diego shipwrights did in hours what it had taken her builders days to do, back in the Isle of Man a century before.

— PHOTO BY AUTHOR

Considering the fact that their hulls were made of reinforced concrete, the steam tankers Cuyamaca and San Pasqual weren't bad looking. Here is the Cuyamaca, ready to be launched sideways, in 1920.

— PHOTO BY AUTHOR

When men put their shoulders against the stem of the little steam tug Emma and pushed her into the bay, back in 1882, no one dreamed that a mile or so away and a mere 83 years later, anything like this would happen. Here is American President Line's cargo liner President Polk sliding into San Diego Bay from the plant of the National Steel & Shipbuilding Co. on Jan. 23, 1965.

— NATIONAL STEEL & SHIPBUILDING CO.
PHOTO, BY KIM LEE

With some 1400 miles of open sea ahead of her, the huge Puget Sound ferryboat Hyak, San Diego-built in 1967, returns to the yard after a trial run outside the harbor. Note the "jury" bow on her lower deck, for protection while boring into head seas of the not-always-too-Pacific.

— NATIONAL STEEL & SHIPBUILDING CO.
PHOTO, BY KIM LEE

"We're sober men and true — And attentive to our duty!" — but when they were not sober, the men of the U.S.S. Ranger had a tendency to re-arrange things in that quaint part of San Diego known as Stingaree. In this photo of around 1885, some of them pose proudly around her muzzle-loading bowgun, a 24-pounder Parrott rifle.

— HISTORICAL COLLECTION,
TITLE INSURANCE & TRUST CO.

Although San Diego was for many years a "destroyer port", the first of those swift warcraft to steam in past Point Loma were British, rather than American; H.M.S. Virago and Sparrowhawk paid a visit, en route to Esquimalt, B.C. from England, late in 1897. Here is the Virago, at anchor off Spreckels' Wharf with her barkentine-rigged escort, H.M.S. Leander, in the background.

— HISTORICAL COLLECTION, TITLE INSURANCE & TRUST CO.

Both speed-cones are up to the yard-arms — "All engines ahead, standard speed" — as the grand old U.S.S. Oregon makes a small bit of Naval history. The first battleship ever to enter San Diego Bay, she is shown here as she steams out past North Island at the end of that notable visit, in the autumn of 1911.

— ASA TAYLOR

The big Spreckels' tug Fearless was taken up by the Navy in 1898, but returned to San Diego many times, as the U.S.S. Iroquois. In the distance, in this 1913 view, are the end of the Coal Bunkers Wharf, the Hawaiian bark Nuuanu, and two unidentified Navy vessels.

— PHOTO BY AUTHOR

Decent of you to ask, Old Chap, but we sha'nt be needing a pilot; not going inside, you know. And so on Dec. 31, 1887, H.M.S. Triumph, *flagship of Rear Adm. Algernon C. F. Heneage, R.N., came to an anchor off San Diego Bay and Capt. Jim Niles ruefully headed for home in the black-hulled pilot-sloop* Restless. *Ah, well — perhaps he could catch a few barracuda, good for four bits each, on his way back to town.*

— HISTORICAL COLLECTION,
TITLE INSURANCE & TRUST CO.

White funnels, long-necked davits, and an ornately-railed "captain's walk" complete with scalloped awning; the French cruiser Protet *is reflected in the placid waters of San Diego Bay in 1901. The trim, white square-rigger in the distance is the British ship* Sierra Blanca.

— HISTORICAL COLLECTION,
TITLE INSURANCE & TRUST CO.

Deep in thought, to say nothing of being bundled up in bridge-coat and beard, Lt. Billy Gunn, Naval Militia of California, sits on a skylight as the U.S.S. Pinta *heads for San Diego in 1897. Too little and too late, she was built as a Civil War tug but wasn't launched until the war was nearly over — so they sent her out to California, converted her into a gunboat of sorts, and for ten years used her as the San Diego headquarters of the Naval Militia. Just under the officer's right elbow in the picture appears one of her two howitzers; the gun mounted just forward of her staff is one of her pair of .45-70 Gatlings.*

— HISTORICAL COLLECTION,
TITLE INSURANCE & TRUST CO.

A dainty little steam barkentine, the U.S.S. Princeton, lies off sparsely-settled Coronado in 1906. The gunboats were small and lightly armed — but mighty handy in those forgotten days when mistreatment of Americans by banana-republic dictators brought swift and effective action.

— HISTORICAL COLLECTION,
TITLE INSURANCE & TRUST CO.

"The Great White Fleet" came to San Diego, in 1908 — but the water still wasn't deep enough for the battleships to get inside the bay. Here is the battleship Illinois, somewhat unique in having her two funnels placed athwartships, like a Mississippi steamboat. Another novelty of design is seen in the New Jersey, astern of her to the left, with her "superimposed" turrets — a brace of 8-inch guns mounted atop two 12s. Off to the right is the Vermont.

— HISTORICAL COLLECTION,
TITLE INSURANCE & TRUST CO.

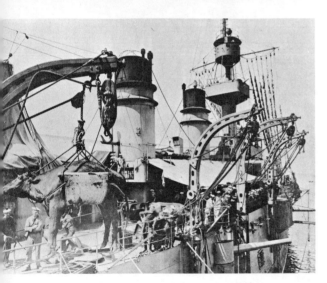

Lowering war-clouds of 1914 caught the French cruiser Montcalm in San Diego Bay — but they let her stay long enough to take on provisions and fresh water. Innocent of bulk refrigeration, she loaded 20 head of steers and 40 of sheep, brought out by the ferryboat Coronado, for a supply of fresh meat. The tent-like canvas affair abaft the second funnel hides two carloads of baled hay, and a further air of domesticity is lent by the week's wash, strung up to her signal-yards.

— HISTORICAL COLLECTION,
TITLE INSURANCE & TRUST CO.

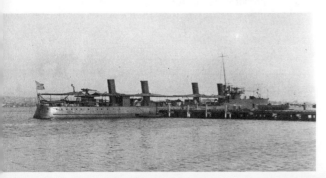

One of our earliest destroyers, the U.S.S. Paul Jones lies at "Torpedo Wharf" on the Coronado side of the bay, about 1912. Coal-burners, with reciprocating engines, it was a big day when one of her class got up to 28 knots — and her single, bare mast reveals that, for her, radio was still in the future.

— PHOTO BY AUTHOR

San Diego's citizen sailors — men of the Third Division, Naval Militia of California, aboard the U.S.S. Alert for a Sunday of drill, in 1903. The mustachioed bluejacket in the second row, far right, is Louis Almgren Jr., later to serve for many years as Chief of the San Diego Fire Department. A branch of the National Guard, the Naval Militia was the forerunner of today's U. S. Naval Reserve.

— DON M. STEWART COLLECTION

Built in England in 1875, the Mexican gunboat Democrata was a frequent visitor to San Diego in the early days. Frequently afflicted with what one of Kipling's characters described as "... copious minor defects in her engineroom," she found her bark-rig useful — although in this 1880 snapshot everything but stays'ls, gaff tops'l and brailed-up spanker seem to have been sent down. Originally she was armed with a 100-pounder muzzle-loading cannon on each side, two 20-pounder breech-loaders and a 6-pounder field-gun.

— DON M. STEWART COLLECTION

Small but swift: the torpedoboat Farragut at San Diego in 1911. She was laid down at the Union Iron Works in 1896 and displaced only 273 tons — but she logged 31.7 knots on her trial run. The third mast in the picture belongs to the U.S.S. Rowan, as do the two horizontal-topped stacks which appear between those of the Farragut; her third stack is just forward of the Farragut's tiny main-mast, and it was easy for her to hide behind another torpedoboat, for she was only a 182-tonner.

— PHOTO BY AUTHOR

A trim little cruiser of the "White Squadron" days — the U.S.S. Chicago, flagship of·the Pacific Squadron and a frequent visitor to San Diego, where she is shown at anchor in 1906. One of the Navy's first vessels to carry wireless, she was midway between San Diego and San Francisco at the time of the earthquake and fire, and served as a "relay station" for disaster traffic, between the then weak transmitters at the two ports.

— HISTORICAL COLLECTION,
TITLE INSURANCE & TRUST CO.

The U.S.S. New York, flagship of Rear Adm. William T. Sampson, helped to make history off Santiago in 1898. Here she is 18 years later, anchored in San Diego Bay — but by then she had become the U.S.S. Saratoga, under the Naval policy to name battleships, and only battleships, after states. She was only a cruiser, having nothing larger than 8-inch guns, and her original name was taken by the super-Dreadnaught New York.

— PHOTO BY AUTHOR

At the outbreak of the First World War, the German gunboat Geier interned at Honolulu. When the United States entered the war she was seized — but not before extensive sabotage had been carried out by her crew. Here we see her a few months later, as the U.S.S. Carl Schurz, anchored in San Diego Bay.

— PHOTO BY AUTHOR

"Did you see the Harvard? She was in, yesterday; just stayed a few hours. All painted up in camouflage — and she's got crow's nests and a searchlight platform and they've built a bridge on top of her pilot-house!" So went that waterfront whisper in 1917 when the old favorite paid a touch-and-go visit to San Diego. What they didn't know was that she was now the U.S.S. Charles and that she was on her way through the Panama Canal and across the Atlantic. She was used on shuttle service across the English Channel, and carried many thousands of American troops to the battlefields of France.

— HISTORICAL COLLECTION,
TITLE INSURANCE & TRUST CO.

In the dazzle comouflage of the First World War the U.S.S. Caldwell, then only a few weeks old, quietly slips out of San Diego Bay in 1918, bound for the European war zone.

— PHOTO BY AUTHOR

By 1929 San Diego's skyline had grown a bit, Middleground Shoal was no more, and the depth of water across the bar was sufficient that battleships now came and went as a routine matter. Here the U.S.S. Texas lies at anchor, off Broadway Pier.

— HISTORICAL COLLECTION,
TITLE INSURANCE & TRUST CO.

When the big battleship New Mexico arrived
in 1919 she was still too big to try getting
into San Diego Bay, but visitors were willing
to go outside to board her. The formally
dressed sightseer, complete with carnation
and velour hat, seems deeply interested in
something just off-camera.

— PHOTO BY AUTHOR

Although she now was twenty years old the
U.S.S. Wasmuth, one of the famous "four-
pipers" of the First World War, seems to be
having no difficulties as she tops 30 knots on
her annual full-power run, off San Diego.

— PHOTO BY AUTHOR

Once a favorite with East Coast vacationers,
the passenger liner Bunker Hill was taken
up by the Navy in the First World War and
became the U.S.S. Aroostook (center) —
nicknamed "Beno" because of a one-time
Executive Officer whose two favorite expres-
sions were "There'll be no liberty" and
"There'll be no boats." To her left is the
transport Chaumont, to her right the light
cruiser Raleigh. About 1935.

— PHOTO BY AUTHOR

How simple and uncluttered was the bridge of a four-pipe destroyer, in those peaceful days of 1920! At standard speed the U.S.S. Anthony returns to San Diego after exercises at sea.

— PHOTO BY AUTHOR

It was a big event for San Diego when the U.S.S. Constitution arrived in 1931, on a tour of West Coast ports, and later returned to spend the winter at Navy Pier. Here she is shown airing her sails — and one look at that monstrous fore tops'l is enough to explain why, in 1856, the single tops'l was discarded and double-tops'ls came in, each about half the area of the old singles. For reasons which were not quite clear the Constitution, after her restoration, never set sail at sea, but journeyed from port to port, ignominiously, at the end of a tow-line. Across the slip from her, at Broadway Pier, are the Panama Pacific liner California and the coastwise freighter Corrales.

— PHOTO BY AUTHOR

The Navy's "Tug Row" at the foot of Ash Street, about 1935. They were all steam, in those days, and that big whistle on the "Indian" class tug Pinola, far left, sounded as impressively as it looked. Astern of her is the fleet tug Sonoma, and then the "Bird" class minesweeper Rail. The four "sweeps" lying outboard, all of them used as tugs or as seaplane- or submarine-tenders, are unidentified.

— PHOTO BY AUTHOR

The lull between two wars: a portion of San Diego's moth-balled fleet of four-pipers, about 1935. In a Herculean operation directed by the late Commo. Byron McCandless, USN, they were hauled out one by one, cleaned up and tuned up, and sent back to sea, both for our own, and for the Royal Navy under lend-lease.

— HISTORICAL COLLECTION, TITLE INSURANCE & TRUST CO.

By 1932, people hardly gave a second glance when vessels as big as the U.S.S. Saratoga, a 33,000-ton aircraft-carrier 888 feet long, came in and anchored. Just beyond her are the buildings of the Naval Air Station on North Island, with Point Loma in the background.

— HISTORICAL COLLECTION,
TITLE INSURANCE & TRUST CO.

The U.S.S. Milwaukee, a 6-inch-gun cruiser, anchored off Coronado about 1912, with the destroyer-tender Iris alongside. Originally the British tramp steamer Dryden and then, briefly, the Menemsha, the Iris was one of the merchantmen we bought when the Spanish-American War caught us, as other wars have done, with ships in short supply. During the First World War the Iris became a training-ship for the U. S. Shipping Board and then was scrapped; the Milwaukee was stranded, off Eureka, in 1917.

— PHOTO BY AUTHOR

To Pacific Mail's side-wheeler Oregon apparently goes the distinction of being the first steamer to enter San Diego Bay; that was on March 30, 1849, and she didn't come in by choice — she came in because if she hadn't, her owners wouldn't have collected their mail subsidy for that voyage. She only stayed thirty minutes and probably wasn't very gracious about it — but then, as of 1847 anyone who wanted San Diego could have had it.

— COURTESY THE MARINERS MUSEUM,
NEWPORT NEWS, VA.

As the Mayflower was to New England, so was the Orizaba to San Diego — "Ah, yes — but my folks came here in the Orizaba!" was enough to put any upstart in his place. This painting by Joseph Lee shows her in the colors of the Pacific Coast Steamship Co. and was sighted in a Seattle sail-loft in 1912; as of 1968 it was still the object of a diligent but fruitless search.

— HISTORICAL COLLECTION,
TITLE INSURANCE & TRUST CO.

Her champagne days as a passenger-liner between San Diego and San Francisco now past, the one-time New York towboat Goliah, her cabins torn away, wound up in Puget Sound towing service, where she lasted until 1894, when she was laid up at Port Ludlow. She was built in 1848 and came out during the Gold Rush; during her passenger service the famous Lt. George H. Derby was a frequent passenger, and she was the one who rescued the passengers from the wrecked Yankee Blade at Point Conception in 1854.

— COURTESY THE MARINERS MUSEUM,
NEWPORT NEWS, VA.

Like the Eureka, the little freighter Bonita was called a "hog-boat" because she frequently carried hogs on the hoof; this trip, however — and it's some time around 1890 — she has a less fragrant cargo, of sacked grain. Note the Chinese junk alongside — and isn't that flat-car the cutest little thing you ever saw?

— HISTORICAL COLLECTION,
TITLE INSURANCE & TRUST CO.

Was it faulty stowage — or were there just too many passengers lining the starboard rail? At any rate this view of the Queen of the Pacific proves that in 1888, San Diego took Steamer Day seriously. A couple of years later the steamer's name was shortened to Queen, and in November of 1907 she made local history by being the first wireless-equipped merchant ship to enter San Diego Bay.

— HISTORICAL COLLECTION,
TITLE INSURANCE & TRUST CO.

They say that there was never another ship which looked like the little Mexican steamer M. Romero Rubio, which perhaps is just as well; her hump-backed sheer appears to have been an afterthought by some naval architect who must have had anti-social tendencies. The steamer in the background is the Orizaba, so it is before Jan. 12, 1887, when that old favorite left San Diego for the last time, to be broken up.

— HISTORICAL COLLECTION,
TITLE INSURANCE & TRUST CO.

It's a raw and foggy afternoon in 1892, and Pacific Mail's City of New York is paying an unwilling call at San Diego. Pressure by Congressman W. W. Bowers made the line resume its calls that year — but when his term was over, so was their San Diego service. The steam "dummy" and its car (foreground) handled passengers and freight on the 1700-foot long Steamship Wharf.

— HISTORICAL COLLECTION,
TITLE INSURANCE & TRUST CO.

Outward bound for Redondo, Port Los Angeles, Santa Barbara and San Francisco, the Santa Rosa passes the end of Pt. Loma, around the turn of the century. An iron, single-screw steamship of 2416 gross tons, she was built at Chester, Pa., in 1884, and was on the San Diego-San Francisco run for more than a quarter of a century. About 1907 her second funnel was removed, which did nothing at all for her appearance; she was wrecked at Pt. Arguello July 7, 1911.

— HISTORICAL COLLECTION,
TITLE INSURANCE & TRUST CO.

An infrequent visitor to San Diego, the Spokane is shown entering the harbor in the late 1890s. In 1922 she was renamed Admiral Rogers, and in 1948 she was sold for scrapping.

— HISTORICAL COLLECTION,
TITLE INSURANCE & TRUST CO.

Old-style, radial davits still were standard equipment when this snap-shot was taken on the Santa Rosa's boat-deck, as she headed north from San Diego in 1903. Incidentally, the little old steamer with her reciprocating engine and single screw was no slow-poke; early in 1887 she made it from San Francisco to San Diego in just under 32 hours.

— AUTHOR'S COLLECTION

Ending the first leg of her voyage from San Diego to Seattle, the majestic steamship Governor passes the Rose City at San Pedro in 1911. Those towering funnels pre-date by many years the era of the liner whose funnel motif is the inverted flower-pot, the oil-well derrick — or the "free-form" whatizzit. Built in 1907, the Governor went down after a collision in Puget Sound April 1, 1921.

— PHOTO BY AUTHOR

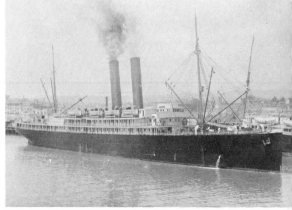

The old Quarantine Station, the original Navy Coaling Station, and North Island, then a mere expanse of sage-brush, from the top of Point Loma about 1913. The steamship is the President, inbound from Puget Sound via San Francisco and Wilmington.

— PHOTO BY AUTHOR

"The table groaned with its load of toothsome viands" — not only in the dining-saloon of the Roanoke, but of all the others calling at San Diego in the days of the passenger ships. As befitted its elite status, the Captain's Table, in the foreground, had far more ornate chairs than did the others. A photo of 1914.

— HISTORICAL COLLECTION,
TITLE INSURANCE & TRUST CO.

Victorian elegance still ran riot in the deluxe, two-berth staterooms of the Roanoke in 1914, even if you did have to pour your own water from a ewer, and call the steward to empty the waste. The little brass fitting on the bunk-rail, near the pillows, with its disposable paper liner, was much appreciated by passengers afflicted with mal-de-mer. The bulkheads are panelled in lincrusta, which was made from canvas and linseed oil, and must have been just great in the event of a fire.

— HISTORICAL COLLECTION,
TITLE INSURANCE & TRUST CO.

Far less ornate, but also less expensive, were the three-berth staterooms in the Roanoke, being done in simple, enameled tongue-and-groove. The number on the berth was inscribed on the passenger's ticket — so get your gear off of my bunk and up into No. 1 where it belongs, Stranger. And don't step on my face when you climb in!

— HISTORICAL COLLECTION,
TITLE INSURANCE & TRUST CO.

Neat, but not gaudy; such was the modest social-hall of the steam schooner Wapama, now restored at San Francisco and the last of her kind. There was no ship's orchestra and the horrors of "planned enjoyment" were far in the future — but a nickle in the coin-operated piano would get you The Oceana Roll or even Alexander's Ragtime Band.

— HARRY DRING

Increased size brought more luxury, and here we have the tavern room of the Panama Pacific liner Virginia, *as she lay at Broadway Pier in 1930. This was, of course, during Prohibition, so all of the bottled-goods had been locked up, and sealed by Customs, as soon as she made San Diego westbound. She would be a dry ship until she left her last California port eastbound, when the seals would be gleefully broken — to go on again at New York.*

— PHOTO BY AUTHOR

West Santa Fe Wharf about 1912. In the foreground is the little Mexican passenger steamer Victoria, *built at Port Townsend as the* Garland *around 1890, and lost in a storm near the Coronado Islands May 1, 1915. Astern of her is the trim little Army steamer* Lieut. George M. Harris.

— BOB NEILL

One of the many "opposition" cargo and passenger steamers which visited San Diego from time to time was the little wooden-hulled Eureka, *shown temporarily laid up at the Coal Bunkers around 1912. She was built at Wilmington, Cal., in 1900 and was wrecked at Point Bonita Jan. 8, 1915.*

— PHOTO BY AUTHOR

A former transatlantic liner, the handsome Finland, *launched from Cramp's yard at Philadelphia in 1902, lies at Broadway Pier in the early 1920s. At that time she was running on the New York-San Francisco service, via Havana, Panama, San Diego and Los Angeles, for the Panama Pacific Line.*

— HISTORICAL COLLECTION, TITLE INSURANCE & TRUST CO.

A busy day at Broadway Pier in 1925. At the far left is Admiral Line's Emma Alexander; *then comes Pacific Mail's old* Mongolia, *then calling at San Diego in Panama Pacific's intercoastal trade, while nestling in a corner of the slip is the little Canadian motorship* Gryme, *which traded down the Lower Coast. Across the slip at B Street Pier is the U.S.S.* Chaumont. *Steam schooner in the distance is unidentified.*

— FRED REIF COLLECTION

Toilers of the sea — or at least, of B Street Pier. It is around 1930 and the freighter is the little steam-schooner Chehalis, *at that time operating as one of the "independents". Of wood throughout, she was built by that master shipwright Hans D. Bendixsen at Fairhaven, Calif., in 1901. Not long after this picture was taken she was laid up in Oakland Creek, never to sail again.*

— PHOTO BY AUTHOR

With a bone in her teeth, the popular Emma Alexander — *ex*-Congress, *ex*-Nanking *and eventually* Empire Woodlark — *heads down the bay from Broadway Pier, around 1920.*

— PHOTO BY AUTHOR

Hey-day of the intercoastal ships; it is 1928, and Panama Pacific's liner California, *on her maiden voyage, is coming alongside Broadway Pier with the help of the Star & Crescent tug* Palomar. *Over at B Street Pier lie two of Quaker Line's intercoastal freighters, the eastbound* Peter Kerr *and, just ahead of her, the westbound* San Anselmo.

— PHOTO BY AUTHOR

Breaking through the early morning overcast, the sun gilds the trunk of a eucalyptus, and the plumes of smoke from the Yale's *funnels as she slips past Ballast Point Lighthouse in this 1929 view. In the distance, just over her pilot-house, is the famed Hotel del Coronado; the jagged black line on the other side of the channel is Zuniga Jetty.*

— HISTORICAL COLLECTION,
TITLE INSURANCE & TRUST CO.

A century of progress; it is July 15, 1963, and the British cruise-ship Oriana, *of P. & O. - Orient Lines, is at Broadway pier. At 41,915 tons, she was the largest merchantmen to enter the harbor and contrasts fantastically with the little* Star of India, *whose 100th birthday was celebrated four months later and who originally was British herself — the emigrant ship* Euterpe.

— SAN DIEGO UNIFIED PORT DISTRICT

UPPER DECK

SALOON DECK

Accommodation Plan of the steamer Ancon.
Those 3-berth staterooms B, C, V and W,
alongside the casing of her walking-beam
engine, must have been pretty grim; would
you prefer one of the other lettered rooms,
right up against the thrashing paddle-wheels?

— HISTORICAL COLLECTION,
TITLE INSURANCE & TRUST CO.

Professional skills as a master
mariner were combined with dry
wit and with ability as a typogra-
pher, in the case of Capt. Edward
Payson Nichols of the Down
Easter Frank Pendleton. *Instead*
of writing to his friends, he hand-
set the Ocean Chronicle *and*
mailed copies—which now are
collectors' items. San Diego
appears to have impressed him
when he called in 1887.

— COURTESY OF
THE PENOBSCOT MARINE MUSEUM,
SEARSPORT, MAINE

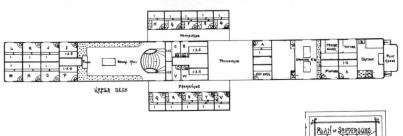

OCEAN CHRONICLE. ---- EXTRA.

PUBLISHED BY *E. P. NICHOLS*, AT SEA, ON BOARD SHIP *FRANK PENDLETON*.

Following Feb. 14.   **SEPT. 19. 1887.**   **NUMBER 14.**

DEAR FRIENDS.

I find the publication of the Ocean Chronicle a failure, as a means of obtaining news from home. From Melbourne I sent seventy copies to Searsport, but have not learned whether they were ever received or not. As I print only for pastime and my own pleasure it will not affect me, only I shall not print so many. This is started as a letter and will probably end with this page. Thanking the few at home who thought of us, and many thanks to the 'Marine Journal' and a few others, I will commence my letter by telling you a little about the city of San Diego.

E. P. Nichols.

SAN DIEGO.

San Diego is situated on the Pacific Ocean in lat. 32 42 N. lon. 117 10W. The harbor of San Diego is one of the finest, and it is only equalled by that of San Francisco. Vessels drawing 22 ft. can safely cross the bar, and with a small outlay they could carry in 27 to 30 ft. The harbor is as well protected as any we ever saw; a natural dock, made by the Almighty. They have over five miles of water-front where wharves can be easily run out to twenty-five feet of water. I think that the outlook for San Diego is very bright, and can see nothing to hinder it from becoming a great commercial port. There is one thing about San Diego as a port for shipping; they do not try to squeeze money out of ships, and though it is not a cheap port, we think it will be the cheapest port on the Pacific Coast as soon as they have the facilities which are fast coming forward. we never did business with more agreeable people.

The climate of San Diego is something wonderful, and without doubt it has no equal for its evenness of temperature. It is never hot there, the thermometer seldom rising above 80°. The nights are cool and agreeable, and a good blanket to draw over you at night is all that is required to produce a good night's rest. It is never cold, the thermometer rarely falling below 40°. The city is well laid out, and when the water is all laid through, as it soon will be, it will be able to produce the most beautiful surroundings to the residences there, for everything will grow, where water can be obtained, and the surrounding valleys bring out a greater variety of fruit and vegetables than can be found in most localities.

Coronado Beach, opposite the city of San Diego about one half mile distant, is a most beautiful location for a seaside resort.. It has a very fine sandy beach for a distance of six miles or more. Four miles of this beach extends from the island — so called — in a narrow strip from two hundred to three hundred feet wide and connects with the main-land about five miles from the Mexican line, thus dividing the Pacific Ocean from the Bay of San Diego making a very fine harbor. The Coronado Beach Co- are erecting a very large hotel which is said to cover seven acres, including the court which is to be an immense garden, around which the hotel is built. The building will contain six hundred rooms and will be opened on the 1st of Dec, next. There is no doubt that a very few years will transform that once 'barren "island" into a large town with magnificent buildings surrounded with beautiful flower-gardens, fruit and shade trees, and everything that grows and beautifies. We own no lot on the Beach; we wish we did; even our good looks failed to bring anyone forward and present us with one.

We tried to get enough money together to buy a lot, but failed to raise enough for a lot on the Beach so we took our $4—all that we could raise—and invested in a lot (tery) in

Louisiania which we think is just as good an investment as some of the "wildcats" outside of San Diego. We should not hesitate to invest—had we the money—anywhere on the Bay of San Diego, but when they go out twenty-five miles all around and cut it up into 25 feet lots, then we have nothing to say, only that we should give Louisiania the preference as an investment.

Ships coming out of San Diego with the wind so far west that she cannot fetch by the Coronados, will find it hard to work off of the beach if the wind is light. We beat all day and then run inside of the Coronados, then we worked off all right. We have said about all we can at present for San Diego, for fear you will think we are running an advertisement, which is not the case. If those interested would make it an object for us we would give a little elasticity to our account, but money cannot hire us to lie —— without it is paid in advance.

AMERICAN SEAMEN.

"The American seamen?" Where are they? They are among the things of the past. The U. S. at present could not furnish seaman to man a fleet (supposing she had one) sufficient to protect the entrance to Boston harbor. It is not an exaggeration to say that nine-tenths of the seamen sailing in American ships, are foreigners without even an "intention" of becoming a citizen. American vessels.-The few that are left—might be supplied with good seamen, and have a class that might properly be called "American seamen" if Government would help in the matter. All the shipping laws enacted since 1871 have been — on the whole—but very little benefit to a ship, seaman, or ship-owner, if we except a part of the Dingley Bill. The Advance Clause is a failure and will never be carried out until Government assists. As the law now is, it is like driving a row of piles at low-water-mark and telling the water that it cannot pass through.

We propose something like the following, to follow the "Tonnage Bill" which would squelch all sailor robbers on shore, give our ships the best seamen, and would protect American sea men, and give them a chance to help themselves. Whereas not over one tenth of the seaman that come into the U. S. would be required for our foreign trade, it would give us a chance to get good men. It should also provide for our coasting vessels which could be done by allowing more wages while actually employed "coasting".

We will here give our idea roughly, and hope some of our friends will improve on it. For want of a name we will call this the

NICHOLS BILL.

Be it enacted by the Senate and House of Representatives of the United States of America in Congress assembled; That the United States Government found a society for the promotion of American Seamen and to build up a Naval Reserve force : that the society so formed shall be known as the "United States Marine and Naval Force," the object of which is to provide ships with seamen at fixed rate of wages, the seamen to have a regular pay from Government, from the time of joining until they cease to be members.

Every sort of importance in the United States shall be provided with accommodations to board and keep sufficient seamen to meet the requirements of American ships which shall be furnished at a fixed and regular pay, the seamen to look to government for all wages.

All American seamen of good character, in good health may join, and seamen of any country who can give good testimonials showing six month's good character, shall be eligible to membership until such a number shall have been made members as shall be deemed sufficient to meet the requirements of the American ships.

Their pay shall be $——, per month from the day they become a member until such time as they cease to be a member, whether employed or unemployed.

Every seaman to be entitled to two days on shore, at the expiration of every voyage for every month he has served, but if circumstances require him to serve sooner, he shall receive remuneration for such time.

All members must board as directed, but in case of a member being near home, or among friends, permission may be given, and allowances made.

U S Consuls shall be empowered to make a limited number of members, and make provision for the maintainance of members in their Dis.

Ships wanting crews shall be furnished with the same by applying to the Government office the ship to be responsible to Government for their wages at $——, per month.

Members showing four years good conduct shall be entitled to citizens papers. Eight years shall entitle them to $— per month extra pay. Fifteen years, shall entitle them to a pension of $—— annually

Bad conduct shall lay the member open for dismissal— at the discretion of Government— at which time his pay shall cease.

* * * * *

This is the rough timber which we hand over to our friends to put through the political saw-mill and pass it over to our legislative carpenters to build upon. Those who talk of building up a navy should remember that it takes seamen as well as ships to make a navy and seamen are the harder to make.

Our space forbids saying more but it is our wish that some one handle this in a better manner and give it a wider circulation than can be given by the OCEAN CHRONICLE.

LOCAL ITEMS.

Sat Aug. 26, sailed from San Diego Cal. for Port Townsend W. T.

The wind was well to the west and took us to lat. 29, when it hauled northerly.

Eleven days out finds us in lat. 42, lon. 144 with the wind north-east and no sign of any westerly wind.

One of our doves went on shore to breakfast just as we were leaving San Diego and did not return to the ship, so lost his passage.

We shall not print the other side of this page but if our San Diego friends wish to use it for advertising just send us a deed of a corner lot and we'll withdraw this and print your "ad". Nothing mean about us.

Sept, 9. An iron ship in sight which we call the "C. S. Bement" but are not sure; she has three sky-sails (masts for,) and six top-gallantsails, She is too far off to signal.

We got up to Cape Flattery Sept, 13, when we had the — — (we refrain). Arrived up to Port Townsend the 16th. We found the ship chartered to load coal at Departure Bay for San Francisco. Arrived Dep. Bay on the 18th.

For a slug of red-eye or a more-or-less gentlemanly game of billiards — or to keep up with current events by perusing the Daily Alta California — all you had to do was to saunter down to the Orizaba Saloon; it was named after the current favorite of the coastwise steamers.

In the late 1860s, Culverwell's Wharf played a vital part in the life of rapidly expanding San Diego.

Whether the steward's department needed pot-roast or mutton-chops, the New Town branch of the San Diego Market was ready and willing, and there was free delivery at dockside or at anchor.

At sea or in port, morning noon or night, the coastwise passenger ships prided themselves on their meals — and there was no limit to the size of your order. For the traveler lacking in self-control, keeping one's weight within reasonable limits could become a problem.

— COLLECTION OF ROBERT W. PARKINSON

Steamers were on a six-day schedule in 1869, when the side-wheelers were at the peak of their glory — and even more frequently, when some "Opposition" operator attempted to muscle into the lucrative trade.

Only slightly higher than the steam schooners were North Pacific's fares, at the time of the 1915 Exposition; they were using the veneran steamships Roanoke *and* George W. Elder. *Meanwhile the Mexican steamers* Benito Juarez *and* Victoria *of the Cia. Naviera del Pacifico S. A. were running down the Lower Coast, and Meteor's little motorship* San Diego *connected with Ensenada and Long Beach.*

— COLLECTION OF JOHN H. ANDERT

There's nothing like a good, rousing rate-war to appeal to free and untrammeled steamship operation; the big boys can stand rate-slashing, the little boys can't, and before long things are back to normal. Tariffs reflected in this 1874 advertisement show clearly that another "Opposition" line had appeared.

— DEL VALLE COLLECTION; L. A. COUNTY MUSEUM OF NATURAL HISTORY

Before Middleground Shoal was removed, there was a dog-leg bend to negotiate just north of Ballast Point — and the only safe time to hit it was high-water slack. On May 22, 1899, the British steamer Belgian King was delayed for an hour, and got to the bend on a strong ebb; she wound up practically in the front yard of Ballast Point Lighthouse. Luckily, there was no damage other than that to the pride of the master and the pilot, and they got her off on the next tide.

— HISTORICAL COLLECTION,
TITLE INSURANCE & TRUST CO.

On Feb. 10, 1901, the German four-masted bark Edmund, leaking like a basket, was towed in to San Diego Bay by the San Francisco tug L. Luckenbach — later well-known as the Defiance — and there was revealed a saga of hardship and frustration which became a classic of West Coast salvage. She had been on the rocks at Santa Rosalia, Baja California, and they floated her nine times before she finally was able to make it to the north.

— HISTORICAL COLLECTION,
TITLE INSURANCE & TRUST CO.

Streaked with coal-dust and ashes, the dead Bennington lies beached in shallow water after the disaster of July 21, 1905, in which three score of her crew perished. After the boiler explosion she started to fill from ruptured sea connections, but quick work by the tug Santa Fe got her out of deep water before her buoyancy was gone.

— HISTORICAL COLLECTION,
TITLE INSURANCE & TRUST CO.

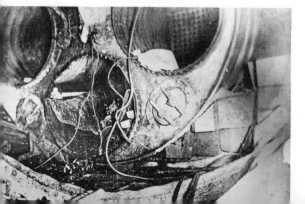

After the explosion. With the boiler-face blown away, the collapsed crownsheet shows plainly in the lower of the three fire-holes.

— COURTESY OF LEE STROEBEL

While a couple of bored officers look on, San Diego firemen pose with their chemical-engine, alongside the burning Alaskan in 1910; note the ventillator, hooded with canvas to shut off air to the smouldering cargo below. This is believed to have been the first shipboard fire to be extinguished — in a sort of a Rube Goldberg way — through the use of CO_2.

— HISTORICAL COLLECTION, TITLE INSURANCE & TRUST CO.

On New Year's Eve of 1909, the lumber-schooner Alice McDonald went on the rocks at the end of Point Loma, during a heavy storm, but was refloated after discharging part of her cargo onto lighters. The tug Bahada is standing by, and the islands on the horizon are Los Coronados, in Mexico.

— CAPT. JOE BRENNAN COLLECTION

Cleaning up the mess. A view on the deck of the gunboat Bennington, after the explosion.

— AUTHOR'S COLLECTION

A landmark passes: The San Diego Boat House, built about 1888, goes up in smoke in 1925. San Diego's then fireboat Bill Kettner, built largely by the firemen themselves, was the first one in the world to be driven by gasoline. She had a 220-horsepower, heavy-duty Atlas — which actually was cut over to less expensive distillate when it got warm — and a pair of 110-horsepower Seagrave fire-truck motors connected to centrifugal pumps.

— PHOTO BY AUTHOR

CAPT. HENRY JAMES JOHNSTON
Steamship *Orizaba*

— HIST. COL., T. I.

CAPT. S. S. DUNNELLS
Steamer *Vaquero; Port Pilot,*
1888-1895

— HIST. COL., T. I.

CAPT. EZEKIEL ALEXANDER
Steamship *Santa Rosa*

— AUTHOR'S COLLECT

"Fun on the Toxteth" was the newspaper heading for a report on the socially and financially successful shipboard bazaar, held aboard the big Cape Horner by the ladies of All Saints' Episcopal Church, as the guests of the captain and his wife. That was in 1902. On March 2, 1908, she left Port Talbot for Tocopilla, and vanished for all time in the gray wastes of the South Pacific.

— FRED REIF COLLECTION

Prelude to tragedy: Capt. David O. (Lucky) Blackburn (just to the right of the wheel) with the ship's company of the British steamer Montserrat, at Babcock & Story's wharf in 1888. At dusk of Dec. 7, 1894 she and another San Diego trader, the Keweenah, both loaded with coal, were sighted, southbound, off Tatoosh Island. They were plunging into a rising storm, and neither of them ever was seen again.

— HISTORICAL COLLECTION,
TITLE INSURANCE & TRUST CO.

CAPT. GORTON A. HARRIS
Steamship Emma Alexander

— PHOTO BY AUTHOR

CAPT. RICHARD C. BRENNAN
Steamship Harvard

— CAPT. JOE BRENNAN COLLECTION

CAPT. FRANK A. JOHNSON
Steamship Yale

— MATSON NAVIGATION C

In its half century and more of operation, the Port of San Diego has had only three men in the post of Port Director, and here they are together in a 1968 photo. To the left are John Bate and Joe Brennan; to the right is Don L. Nay, the present director of the far-flung activities of the Unified Port District.

COURTESY OF UNION-TRIBUNE PUBLISHING CO.

In the 1880s and again in 1915, the steamship George W. Elder was important in the passenger trade to San Diego. In this 1888 view, unfortunately, none of her officers is identified except the Freight Clerk, at the far right — S. T. Johnson, later to serve for many years as the Pacific Steamship Company's agent at San Diego, and a leader in the community.

— HISTORICAL COLLECTION,
TITLE INSURANCE & TRUST CO.

Uniformed officers and a spic-and-span crew; Capt. Lorenzen, the mates, and the rest of the ship's people, aboard the German four-masted bark Lisbeth at San Diego in June of 1909. On the deck below, just forward of the capstan, is one of her Jarvis brace-winches — a man-saving device carried by many of the big steel "four-posters" of the final days of sail.

— HISTORICAL COLLECTION,
TITLE INSURANCE & TRUST CO.

A ship without a country, the old steam whaler Narwhal went Moby Dickish in her old age (those snail-horn davits are both Hollywood and plywood) and finally was towed from Ensenada to San Diego in the early 1930s, when her ownership and registry had become so confused that no one was sure of anything more than her bare existence. On the mudflats near National City, she slowly fell apart.

— PHOTO BY AUTHOR

Disaster at Arguello. In a patchy fog, shortly before dawn on May 30, 1931, the San Diego-bound Harvard made her last and most positive landfall at what has been aptly termed "The Graveyard of the Pacific", all of her 635 people were saved. On her way out to California in 1910, the Harvard set a communications record by sending a wireless message to Coney Island, N.Y., when she was off Manzanillo, Mex., 3,000 miles away. During the First World War she was a troop transport, doing shuttle service across the English Channel, as the U.S.S. Charles.

— HISTORICAL COLLECTION,
TITLE INSURANCE & TRUST CO.

No, Junior, Mr. Bailey is not entertaining the Smith Brothers — or Weber & Fields. Each of the two hands-in-pockets gentlemen probably is the master of a lumber-schooner, or maybe even a barkentine, for Bob Bailey's Bank Exchange was a favorite resort of captains and mates, in the 1890s. The whale-jaws no doubt came from Capt. Enos Wall's try-works on North Island, and it's too bad that you can't see inside; over the back-bar was a fine set of deer antlers, the gift of Capt. Frederick Fardelius of the Bertha Dolbeer.

— HISTORICAL COLLECTION,
TITLE INSURANCE & TRUST CO.

For taking care of unfriendly Indians, the "secret weapon" of the lighthousetender Shubrick was a perforated pipe which could emit a curtain of scalding water, around her guard-rail. America's first steam-powered tender, she came in past Point Loma for the first time May 21, 1858, on her way around from the East Coast where she had been built the year before. She also was the first lighthouse-tender to be operated by the government on the West Coast.

Just as the National Park Service, honest historians, and the better element of "the media" were beginning to break the habit of calling it "The Old Spanish Lighthouse", the 1969 bicentennial of California started to jell, and a prominent local official was among those who began calling it Spanish again. Actually, Old Point Loma Light was built by two Baltimore Irishmen, for the United States government, after California had been admitted to the Union, and Spanish rule had ended more than half a century before. Southern California's first lighthouse, it was first lighted on the night of Nov. 15, 1855.

— SOCIETY OF CALIFORNIA PIONEERS,
SAN FRANCISCO

Established Aug. 1, 1890, Ballast Point Light Station was a fine example of "railroad Gothic" and lasted until 1966, when it was replaced by a light on top of a slender steel tower, and new quarters were built for the Coast Guard personnel who maintain it. The original lantern and the sixth order fixed white lens, ground in France by Saulter-Le Monnier, is preserved at the Cabrillo National Monument, surrounding the old lighthouse on top of Point Loma.

— PHOTO BY AUTHOR

Low clouds frequently obscured Old Point Loma Lighthouse, so the new one — colloquially referred to as "The Lower Light" — was built in a more suitable location, and went into commission March 30, 1891. Its third-order, revolving white lens was ground by Henri Le Paute, in Paris, and originally was illuminated by a kerosene lamp with three concentric, circular wicks. In 1911 it was converted to kerosene vapor, and since 1926 has been electric.

— PHOTO BY AUTHOR

"*The engineers, they are a joke — they fill the ocean full of smoke,*" goes an old Navy song; in this case, however, the Army's trim Lieut. Geo. M. Harris is smoking solely for the benefit of the photographer. Classified as an Artillery Steamer, she handled passengers and supplies between San Diego and Fort Rosecrans, whose buildings appear directly astern of her, and also towed targets. After years of faithful service she was sold, was cut down to Diesel propulsion, and became the Seattle tug *Andrew Foss*.

— CAPT. JOE BRENNAN COLLECTION

Ballast Point — and a lot of history, for this probably is about where Cabrillo landed in 1542. In this 1910 view we see the four 10-inch disappearing guns of Battery Wilkeson, dropped out of sight behind the concrete blast-apron. Just beyond the furthest one is the semi-circular emplacement of Battery Fetterman, built over the ruins of the Spanish fort which, in 1803, engaged the fleeing American brig *Lelia Byrd*. Whalers had their try-works here in the early days of American occupation, but later moved across the channel to Whalers' Bight, which shows just above the lighthouse. In the background are North Island, San Diego and the distant mountains.

— COURTESY OF
COL. GEORGE RUHLEN, U.S.A. (RET.)

It wasn't every lighthouse-tender that carried a presidential suite — but the old *Sequoia* had one, in that big deck-house abaft her main-mast. It was added in 1923 for use by President Warren G. Harding on an Alaskan cruise, and she was standing by in San Francisco when he died. She served San Diego for many years; this 1940 photo shows her after the Coast Guard absorbed the Lighthouse Service, lighthouse-tenders became buoy-tenders, and lighthouses became light-stations.

— PHOTO BY AUTHOR

Believed to have been taken around 1898, this photo shows the Revenue Cutter *Thomas Corwin* in holiday dress. In the background are a "full dressed" four-masted bark, and one of San Diego's Chinese junks. The first government vessel built in Oregon, the *Thomas Corwin* was launched at Albina August 23, 1876, and frequently wintered in San Diego.

— HISTORICAL COLLECTION,
TITLE INSURANCE & TRUST CO.

Built and engined by the Risdon Iron Works, the ferry Ramona came down from San Francisco under her own power and went into service early in July of 1903. She was San Diego's first oil-burning ferry, and the first of any of the local harbor craft to be equipped with electric lights.

— CAPT. JOE BRENNAN COLLECTION

After twenty-six years of faithful service, San Diego's first real ferry, the sidewheeler Coronado is hauled up on the Marine Railway at North Island in 1912 for a much needed scrubbing and repainting.

— PHOTO BY AUTHOR

The Star & Crescent Boat Co.'s Golden West came to San Diego shortly after she was built, at Alamitos Bay in 1908. She served on the Point Loma ferry run, as an excursion-boat and, for a few hectic days in 1914, as a "passenger liner" to Ensenada, Mex., while the regular steamer was laid up. Later she was cut down to a tug.

— HISTORICAL COLLECTION,
TITLE INSURANCE & TRUST CO.

Joseph Supple, later an important figure in shipbuilding on the Columbia, built the little ferry steamer Roseville for the Point Loma Land & Town Co. in 1888, and she boasted not only plush upholstery but, of all things, a piano. For a few years she provided passenger service from San Diego to Roseville, Fort Rosecrans and Ballast Point. Then she was sold; sponsons and upper deck were torn away, and she ended her days as a tug in Central America.

— HISTORICAL COLLECTION,
TITLE INSURANCE & TRUST CO.

San Diego's last steam ferryboat was the Morena, *built in 1920 and laid up 18 years later. During the Second World War the Navy mounted a gun on her, and used her for the "dry run" training of Armed Guard crews for merchantmen. In 1946, shortly after this picture was taken, she was towed away to San Quintin, Baja California, where she ended her days as a storage-hulk.*

— PHOTO BY AUTHOR

When she came out in 1929, San Diego & Coronado's ferry Coronado *was the first Diesel-electric ferry on the bay — and the first propeller-driven one since the Silver Gate fiasco of 1888. Built by the Moore Drydock Co. at Oakland, she is of 502 tons, and rated at 1000 horsepower. This 1968 view was taken from the open-deck* Crown City, *San Diego's last ferryboat.*

— PHOTO BY AUTHOR

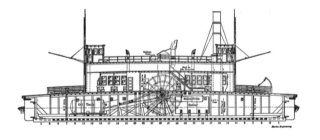

Inboard profile, and midship section of the Ramona. *Her hump-backed sheer, a device to get the driveway over the shaft, presented no problems, and in fact did not detract from her appearance. Her open upper deck was popular with passengers, and she served faithfully until 1929.*

— COURTESY OF
SOCIETY OF NAVAL ARCHITECTS AND
MARINE ENGINEERS

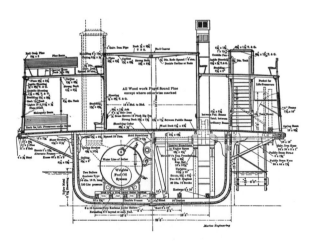

The "nickle-snatcher" ferry Glorietta, of Star & Crescent's North Island service, with a school excursion aboard. In the background are the company's tugs and gasoline-barge, two nests of destroyers, and the North Island Naval Air Station.

— UNION-TRIBUNE PHOTO

The last of San Diego's ferries. In this 1969 view the Crown City, with only a few months left to run, brings a load of automobiles across the bay from San Diego. Built in 1954, she could handle 70 automobiles at a time.

— PHOTO BY AUTHOR

San Diego has always been a push-over for pageants, especially if they have, or can be equipped with, a Spanish angle. So here we are back in 1892; they're celebrating Cabrillo's 150th anniversary, and using one of the local Chinese fishing-junks to portray his caravel. The young man at the left of the group in the foreground obviously buys his collars seriously, and the nice old gentleman in bowler and chin-curtains certainly lends dignity — but the lady with the parasol, out in that wherry, is going to be in deep trouble if it comes on to blow.

— HISTORICAL COLLECTION,
TITLE INSURANCE & TRUST CO.

Around the turn of the century, with the girls of the Zlac Rowing Club out in their barge. In the background is the Dolphin, a veteran charter boat, the sloop Restless and, over toward North Island what appears to be the U. S. S. Hartford, after her reduction to bark rig.

— HISTORICAL COLLECTION,
TITLE INSURANCE & TRUST CO.

At the foot of D Street (now about Broadway and Pacific Highway) around the turn of the century; the dashing character in duck pants and wide-brim Panama no doubt is planning to escape some wild night in a lugger — conveniently at hand, in the foreground. Shortly afterward the Corinthian was absorbed by the San Diego Yacht Club, founded in the 1880s.

— HISTORICAL COLLECTION,
TITLE INSURANCE & TRUST CO.

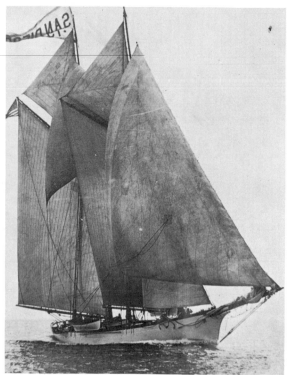

The schooner yacht Lurline served San Diego well; she brought John D. Spreckels to San Diego in the late Eighties and he stayed as a developer even after the great boom collapsed, and in 1912 she won the Honolulu Race for the San Diego Yacht Club. Later sold Mexican, she ended her days as a trader in the Gulf of California.

— HISTORICAL COLLECTION,
TITLE INSURANCE & TRUST CO.

Even before it was completed in 1968, they were using the Twenty-fourth Street Terminal at National City — as witness the heaps of scrap metal on the corner of the pier at the extreme left, and the lumber piled around the warehouse in the center. Kimball's old wharf, where sailing vessels unloaded the port's first heavy cargo eighty-eight years before, was at the foot of Seventeenth Street, just off the picture to the left.

— SAN DIEGO UNIFIED PORT DISTRICT

BIBLIOGRAPHY

ADAMSON, ROBERT: "Point Loma's Century of Light", in *S.D. Historical Society Quarterly*, October 1955.

BRACKETT, R. W.: *The Romantic History of San Diego County Ranchos;* San Diego, 1947.

BRETT, HENRY: *White Wings—Fifty Years of Sail in the New Zealand Trade;* Auckland, N.Z., 1924.

BROWN, GILES T.: *Ships That Sail No More;* Lexington, Ky., 1966.

CHAPMAN, CHARLES E.: *A History of California: The Spanish Period;* New York, 1921.

CUTLER, CARL C.: *Greyhounds of the Sea;* Annapolis, Md., 1961.

DANA, R. H. JR.: *Two Years Before the Mast* (revised edition) Los Angeles, 1960.

FAIRBURN, WILLIAM ARMSTRONG: *Merchant Sail;* Center Lovell, Me., 1945-55.

[FIREMEN'S FUND INSURANCE CO.]: *Firemen's Fund Register;* San Francisco, 1909.

HEILBRON, CARL (ed.): *History of San Diego County;* San Diego, 1936.

JANE, FRED T.: *Fighting Ships;* London, 1911.

KEMBLE, JOHN HASKELL: *The Panama Route;* Berkeley, Cal., 1943.

[LLOYD'S REGISTER OF SHIPPING]: *Lloyd's Register;* London, 1881 and 1915.

LYMAN, JOHN: *The Sailing Vessels of the Pacific Coast and their Builders, 1850-1905;* New York, 1941.

LYTLE, WILLIAM M.: *Merchant Steam Vessels, 1807-1868;* Mystic, Conn., 1952.

MACARTHUR, WALTER: "The Red Record", in *Coast Seamen's Journal*, San Francisco, 1898; *Last Days of Sail on the West Coast*, San Francisco, 1929.

MASON, WILLIAM A.: *Strandings and Wrecks of Vessels on the Coasts of California, Oregon and Washington* (chart); San Pedro, Calif., 1939.

MATTHEWS, FREDERICK C.: *American Merchant Ships, 1850-1890;* Salem, Mass., 1930.

MCNAIRN, JACK, AND MAC MULLEN, JERRY: *Ships of the Redwood Coast;* Stanford University, Calif., 1945.

MILLS, JAMES: *Historical Landmarks of San Diego County;* San Diego, 1959.

NICHOLS, E. P.: *The Ocean Chronicle;* Searsport, Me., 1941.

ROLLE, ANDREW F.: "William Heath Davis and the founding of American San Diego", in *California Historical Society Quarterly*, XXXI, 1; San Francisco, 1952.

RUHLEN, GEORGE: "Fort Rosecrans, California", in *S.D. Historical Society Quarterly*, October 1959.

[SAN DIEGO UNIFIED PORT DISTRICT]: *History and Development of the Port of San Diego* (manuscript); San Diego, n. d.

SHEPARD, TIM: "Yippee! There Went the Tunaboats to War", in *The San Diego Union*, Aug. 6, 1967.

SMYTHE, WILLIAM E.: *History of San Diego;* San Diego, 1906.

SOLOMON, C. R. V.: "Retrospection", in *Sea Breezes;* Liverpool, January through December, 1965.

STEWART, DON M.: *Frontier Port* [San Diego]; Los Angeles, 1966.

[U. S. DEPT. OF COMMERCE & LABOR]: *U. S. Coast Pilot, Pacific Coast* and *U. S. Coast Pilot 7, Pacific Coast;* Washington, D.C., 1909 and 1963; *List of Merchant Vessels of the United States,* Washington, D.C., 1888, 1890, 1906, 1928 and 1950.

WHEELOCK, WALT: *Ferries of the South;* Glendale, Cal., 1964.

WRIGHT, E. W. (ed.): Lewis & Dryden's *Marine History of the Pacific Northwest;* Portland, Ore., 1895.

ZIMMERMAN, ROBERT: "The Four-Pipers: Heroes Through 2 World Wars", in *The San Diego Union,* Mar. 5, 1967.

Additionally, various copies in the following newspaper files: *San Diego Herald,* 1853; *Daily Alta California* (San Francisco, 1850, 1853 and 1865; *The San Diego Union,* 1868 to date.

INDEX

ABBREVIATIONS:

RIG—bg, brig; bk, bark; bkn, barkentine; fer, ferry; ms, motorship; sch, schooner; shp, ship; str, steamer; tkr, tanker; tun, tunaboat. Number "4" preceeding rig denotes 4—mast vessel—i.e., 4bk is four-masted bark.

NATIONALITY—Br, British; Ca, Canadian; Chil, Chilean; Fr, French; Ge, German; Mx, Mexican; Ru, Russian; Sp, Spanish. USS denotes vessel of U. S. Navy; HMS vessel of British Navy. Nationality U. S. if not otherwise indicated.

2758